CHINA BODY AND SOUL

CHINA BODY & SOUL

CONTRIBUTIONS BY

Laurence Binyon

Roger Fry

E. R. Hughes

Innes Jackson

Prof. H. J. Laski

Basil Mathews

Prof. Gilbert Murray

Russell Pasha, etc.

Prof. Eileen Power

Sir Arthur Salter

Arthur Waley

EDITED BY ERNEST RICHARD HUGHES

Essay Index Reprint Series

113233

BOOKS FOR LIBRARIES PRESS

FREEPORT, NEW YORK

First Published 1938
Reprinted 1970

STANDARD BOOK NUMBER:

8369-1661-1

LIBRARY OF CONGRESS CATALOG CARD NUMBER:

78-117811

PRINTED IN THE UNITED STATES OF AMERICA

TABLE OF CONTENTS

5

EDITOR'S PREFACE

IN a book such as this there can be no ordered
progression of thought leading to final
conclusions. I have, therefore, after some
ineffectual efforts at arrangement, decided to cut
the Gordian knot by using an alphabetical order.
Having done that, I invite the reader to enjoy
the privilege of his freedom. Choose the essay
which appeals to you most, and so go back and
forth as you will through the pages of the book.
You will find, as I did when I read the various
manuscripts in the haphazard order of their
arrival, that the very individuality of each study
brings you in the end to a sense of China as a
fact : something, that is, which a man can see
in relation to himself, homely, rational, of the
nature of flesh and blood, but something also of
the spiritual order, built out of ineluctable
dreams which are as impressive as they are
beyond rule-of-thumb interpretation.

The contributors to this book will forgive me if I say a word about them. True generosity is always characterised by its spontaneity, and it is here proved again by the quickness with which those who were approached responded to the appeal. There is pity here for China in her lamentable case, since the proceeds of the book will go to the relief of distress. But respect even more than pity is the key to the spirit of the writing. Those of us who have spent much of our lives in the study of this and that side to Chinese culture, know that we have received something of great price. We have a debt of the spirit which we would pay as best we can. To all of us has come the sober realisation that the lot has fallen to the Chinese people of being a test case. By the way they endure or fail to endure they contribute, to an incalculable degree, to the good or evil fortune of the other peoples in the world.

The history of so old a people as the Chinese is bound to reveal all sorts of phases, militarist and imperialist as well as others. But taking that history as a whole over its range of three thousand years, we find that no nation can compare with them in the scantness of respect they have paid to the power of armed force. And yet on their shoulders is now laid the burden of the world's folly as it breaks out in international schisms. It is not because China is more to blame than any one of the other nations. On the contrary, it is a clear case of vicarious suffering, as the theologians call it. The fathers have eaten sour grapes and the children's teeth are set on edge ; and sometimes we see one race giving this fatal twist to the nexus of cause and effect and itself coming off lightly whilst another race altogether suffers the full force of the consequences.

We turn our eyes on Japan. That she who had commanded our respect, should do what she is doing, is to us the most poignant of tragedies. Our response cannot but be one of settled revolt against the barbarity of her act. But we go further than this. As we face the " new Japan," raw, brutal, shameless in her egoism and palpable mask of deception, we know now, as never before, how easily the path from savagery to civilisation may also become the broad road from civilisation back to savagery. With the Japanese flag of honour being torn to shreds by those specially called to be its guardians, what of our flags of honour in the West? We so easily hypnotise ourselves with our own forms of bushido, the bushido which at one end of the moral scale is so like the chivalry of our Sir Philip Sidney and at the other end is an atavism, a relic of the old ravening beast in man.

The Japanese Army thinks it is winning all along the line, as it fights for the mastery of China's body and soul. It has even dared to celebrate its triumphs : this in spite of the

normal Japanese terror of appearing ridiculous.
But it is only the first phase of the war which
is over, the phase which the Chinese themselves
visualised as only too likely to end as it has.
The second phase now begins, and this is likely
to be a very different one to the first. Certain
factors which so far—— But this preface is
not the place to discuss these issues. What I
would point out is that if China should reduce
her enemies to a willynilly retirement from the
soil they can ravage but not control, the upshot
will be a very subtle humiliation for Japan.
For the China of to-day has shown by her people's
dignity and fortitude that she is the China of the
ages. *That* China learnt in a hard school to treat
an enemy with generosity, with the urbanity
which alone makes it possible to have a return
to peace. I do not say the Chinese will forget
what they have been made to endure. They will
not forget. But once it is clear that China can
only be ruled by her own chosen leaders, those
leaders may be expected to *give* some of those
very privileges Japan is trying to *grab*. It is a
very old idea in China that in the long run it is
wiser to be a gentleman, even though you have
suffered cruelly at the hands of your enemy.

To Miss Innes Jackson the book also owes
its debt. It was a fiery letter from her which
brought home to me that the book must be
done. Then when it came to the essaying of

the task, Miss Jackson gave continuously of her time in acting as secretary to the enterprise.

EDITOR.

INTRODUCTION

Gilbert Murray

THESE essays, written by various persons possessed of special knowledge, serve to lift, here and there, the veil which makes dim for most of us the stupendous tragedy now proceeding to its end in the Far East. They help us to realise the priceless philosophic and æsthetic riches of the Chinese tradition, all the more valuable to us Europeans because so different from our own Græco-Roman heritage. They help us also to appreciate the immense moral and intellectual effort made by the leaders of China in our own day to reduce a vast and bottomless chaos into something like civil order and bring to something like approximate fulfilment the noble testament of Sun Yat-sen.

I speak of a tragedy, but there are really three tragedies. A tragedy of mere suffering and horror, changing and deepening from day to day; of this the book says little or nothing. We read of it, of some small fragment of it, in the daily Press.

It is the ordinary suffering of war, to which we are growing day by day more accustomed, but to which we must resolutely refuse to become accustomed if any humanity is to remain in the human race. Perhaps not quite a war like other wars, being greater in extent than most, numbering by the hundred thousand its dead, dead and unburied, by the million its wounded, wounded and left in agony without tendance; and behind the lines its trains of innumerable refugees, starving, shelterless, and mown down by bombing aeroplanes. The only thing like it that has been seen in Europe, and that on a much smaller scale, was probably at the capture of Malaga, a scene which has been described by two separate British eye-witnesses as surpassing in horror anything they had imagined possible.

A tragedy of marred and blasted hopes. China seemed like a nation reborn after its years of trouble, its ancient culture renovated by contact with the West and still more by the inspiration of its own idealist revolution. There was a movement of hopeful progress everywhere; a new national patriotism, new conceptions of public spirit, a beginning of scientific agriculture, a first understanding of the elements of public health, a great increase in numbers and improvement in standard among University students: all the signs of a great renaissance which seemed likely both to save the exquisite culture which had been the best side of the traditional China and to redeem those disease-stricken and half-starving multitudes that were its worst. A great hope was there, not for China only, but for the future of humanity, since the contribution of China to the intellectual and artistic riches of the world has not yet been fully utilised.

A tragedy of human nature, distorted and depraved. Japan was a noble nation, a nation notable for courage and honour, recently accepted into the circle of great powers ; a trusted member of the Council of the League of Nations, and believed to be a firm pillar of that new edifice of international aspiration which still forms the only hope of the civilised world. And now Japan is a nation dishonoured, a false friend, a breaker of treaties, a people fallen back to barbarism, never to be trusted again. No doubt the Japanese had legitimate requirements, they had grievances. The grievances had been carefully and sympathetically studied by the Lytton Commission, and the effective remedies set forth for public discussion. The changes required could all have been obtained by honourable and peaceful means, and, more, they were real remedies. They would have removed the troubles. As it is the Japanese militarists have preferred other means, of which one hardly knows whether they are more delusive or more devilish ; by blood and lies, by massacre and torture, to make the Chinese love them and buy their goods and so to begin their domination of Asia ! To see to what crimes the gospel of militarism may lead a noble nation, one need only read the report of Russell Pasha on the Japanese encouragement of the Opium Traffic. It is of course a breach of treaty, an offence against humanity—to the militarist that does not matter ; to him the advantage is primarily that it brings illegal gains to the army, but also that it ruins Chinese finances, wrecks the nation's hopes, and undermines the character and self-respect of the Chinese masses, and thus will make the invader's task easier. And what issue is possible from all this infliction of evil ? The best issue would be a financial crisis in Japan, leading to a change of government and a change of policy. Otherwise, if Japan wins, the future is a series of ruinous and inconclusive wars with Russia ; if Japan stays lost in the morass of her own too vast undertaking, China will be first disorganised and then, after long disorganisation, at last militarised, and taught that in a world which shows to the innocent neither mercy nor justice nothing is of value except bombs and poison gas.

Japan had a soul once : can it ever be found again ?

* * *

The purpose of this little book is to gain contributions to the fund for the relief of distress in

China. If we could see for ten minutes some half-mile of the roads behind Shanghai or Nanking we should give all we could afford and more. We must try to help : yet we know that all that this country could possibly give, added to the seventy thousand pounds already collected here, the hundred thousand contributed by the League of Nations and whatever sums may come from America will scarcely satisfy a small fraction of that immense need. The League ambulance units are working nobly ; missionaries, Catholic and Protestant, European and American, are facing hardship and danger as they have always done. We can help them a little with our gifts.

But the best we can do by these means is to ease some parts of the pain of the great tragedy, which ought never to have occurred and need never have occurred. It has occurred because the world in general has not yet learned the lesson of the Great War, now embodied in the Covenant of the League of Nations, that if the vast majority of mankind want peace and law they can obtain their wish by standing firmly together and recognising that an attack on one is an attack on all. This country, I have reason to believe, is ready to take whatever collective action certain other great nations can be persuaded to take. In the meantime wars will continue, horrors worse than the Chinese horror will

B

threaten all of us, so long as we fail to accept in our practical life the principle of human brotherhood, so long as we go on, time after time, in one instance after another, betraying the innocent in order to save our own skins.

A TRIBUTE TO THE GENIUS OF CHINESE PAINTING

Laurence Binyon

YEARS ago I remember meeting a man who had been in Peking during the Boxer troubles. The thing that had most impressed him was this : In the chaos of the streets, among the smouldering fires and the litter of destruction, someone had hung up a scroll freshly inscribed in bold Chinese characters with the words : " Out of a Thousand Calamities rises the Everlasting Peace." No " Up with this " or " Down with that," but a proclamation of faith in the things that outlast the cruelties and insanities of man.

To Western temperaments such a gesture may savour of futility and helplessness. Their instinct is to be doing something; to resist, not to acquiesce. No country has suffered more calamities than China ; violence of Nature, floods and famine, devastations by internal wars, slaughter and havoc by invaders from without. But China, the essential China, has always in the end emerged from these ravages, and turned again to

her instinctive pursuits, her immemorial pre-
occupation with the labours and the arts of
peace. So at least it has been in the past.

I write these few lines as a tribute of gratitude
to China for the deep joy, refreshment, and
exhilaration I have got from Chinese painting.
How astonished and incredulous people in England would have been if one had used such
words forty years ago! But now, since the
Chinese Exhibition at Burlington House, there
must be a great many for whom Chinese art has a
real fascination.

Chinese painting gives us something different
from the painting of other countries. And I
suppose the difference springs mainly from this :
that in China painting has been a passion rather
than a profession. The external demand, " what
the public wants," has left less impression on
this art than on any other. The Chinese painters
therefore communicate with an exceptional freedom their personal choice and aim, their pleasure
in the things that delight them most. There are,
of course, the Buddhist paintings, and the
Buddhist Church was as liberal a promoter and
patron of art as the Christian Church has been in
Europe ; there were also pictures made to win
the favour of emperors and to please the taste of
courts. But it is not of specifically religious or
courtly art that we think when Chinese painting
is spoke of ; still less of portraiture, which bulks

so largely in the art of Europe. Wang Wei, if I remember rightly, the famous painter and poet of the eighth century, had his portrait painted sitting in a chair with his back to the spectator; and that seems symbolic of the Chinese artist's attitude. What we think of, rather, is great prospects over lake or estuary, remote peaks rising out of mist, plunging waterfalls; and bamboos bending to the wind, and twisted pines on crags; and flowers, perhaps flowers above all, with birds flitting about them or perching on the sprays. As I write snow is falling, it has covered all the trees, little cakes of it crumble down from the branches. And I think of the Chinese adoration of the beauty of snow, and how they cherish the first blossoms that appear before the snows have gone. I remember that there were painters who devoted their whole lives to the painting of the prunus-blossom.

It is not so much then the ordered harmony of a complex composition such as, in European masterpieces, invites us to dwell on the fullness of mass and tone, the beauty of the transitions, the magical glow of chosen colour, the whole fabric of form inexhaustible in its richness; it is not so much this that commands our admiration as something more intimate and elusive. For many a Chinese painting, in which the cold eye finds but an arbitrary slightness, becomes, in the mind that can welcome it, something more than itself. It is as if it would step softly into that mind, saying : " I am nothing." But, as water poured over the hands will sometimes evoke a sense of that element as strangely alive, and suddenly perhaps induce a consciousness of the wonder of fluidity, and how the streams wander the world and the seas change from sleep to fury and from fury to sleep, and how the water mingles with everything, and spreads and hides, conquers and yields ; so the little painting may efface itself as if in deprecation, and yet have whispered something in the ear in passing ; it has dropped a seed which in the mind that receives it will spring and expand. For it has come from another mind, another sensibility, which, though a thousand years may have passed since the painter's hand crumbled into dust, needs only the response of an understanding eye to awake and live. A naked tree, a bank and misty water ; or a reed-bed where the wild geese are ; it may be nothing more than these, or even less, that is on the silk or paper, evoked with brief touches ; but if we are submissive and receptive, we become one with the painter and somehow subtly share the feeling which prompted him to take his brush and through so slight a symbol admit us to his world.

There are other paintings which are grand in scale, and are less shy of approach. They indeed invite us, as with a beckoning finger, to enter them. We take a step, the ground is solid beneath our feet; we have left everything behind. Where will this path lead us that disappears beyond that boulder? We mount; suddenly the roar of a torrent meets us; we linger on the wooden, narrow bridge to watch its ruffled haste. Now we are in the heart of the hills; but still the path leads on, higher and higher, breaking open wider and wider prospects; pines stand up in clusters, rooted in seemingly impossible places; clouds float about them; the path gently descends winding about among great rocks and trees; there is a glimmer of brightness; it is the bay of a lake, smooth in sunny mist, and by the water's edge sits a fisherman absorbed in his angling. We have all time to wander in. The scene melts and changes as we descend or climb. High on the hill-slope is a little pavilion, and in it is a poet lost in contemplation. We ascend again into the mountains, into the thinner air. May we not meet, who knows? an Immortal, in ragged disguise, smiling, on his way to those aerial mountain terraces where the Faery Queen holds her court? We are lost in the clouds, all becomes fantastic; then magically the vapour disperses. The path is still before us, leading on and on. There is no end.

Whether we welcome the painting, or the painting welcomes us, what the painter has been concerned with is the transmission of life. Every stroke is to communicate the living, sensitive, elusive essence that made the painter's blood quicken and concentrated itself in the movements of his wrist. How many legends tell of forms painted with such prodigious intensity of creative effort that with the last stroke of the brush they assumed actual life and flew away! There is the legend of the master of masters, Wu Tao-tzü, who led the Emperor to view his last picture, a vast landscape in fresco, and who stepped within his picture, to be seen no more, while the landscape vanished from the wall.

Life! But it has been made a reproach to the Sung painters, devoted to painting hills and streams and clouds, and solitary sages sitting among them, that they turned their backs on life. They were all for escape. Escape from what? From courts and ceremonies, from the routine of offices, and also from the savage excitements and brutalities of war. It is true that the Chinese deeply felt the humiliation of the Mongol conquest, and the loss of the northern provinces. But the instinct which led them to seek life, the refreshment and enhancement of life, in stream and forest and mountain air, had been there also in earlier times, in the flush of material glory. Let us suppose that the painters had turned their backs on the things in which they really delighted and had made their themes of battle and bitterness. Should we have gained?

We should certainly have lost an expression of
human sensibility unique of its kind. And surely
the painters, in making such a choice, would
have left unexpressed the Chinese soul.

" Escape " is a word that has become a parrot
cry of critics. I would substitute another word :
" Liberation." Let me recall a picture which
was lent to the Burlington House exhibition by
the Chinese Government, and which those who
saw it must surely have been drawn to again and
again. I mean the picture of Deer in Autumn
Woods, assigned, probably with good reason, to
the tenth century, between the dynasties of T'ang
and Sung. To look at this picture was to be
transported into it. Invisibly one could step into
those woods, with the still thick foliage of
crimson and tarnished silver, and be among the
shy gracefully-moving deer without putting them
to flight by rude intrusion. The painter has
seemed himself to share their life in those leafy
solitudes ; he recognises their dignity no less
than their beauty. There is no thought of pur-
suing and killing ; it is enough to contemplate
and understand. And to be freed from that
hunting and killing instinct, is not that truly a
liberation, though no doubt to the majority of
mankind the instinct is a natural and a laudable
one ? " Production without possession, action
without self-assertion, development without
domination " ; this is the character, according to

Lao-tzü, of the creative spirit of the universe. And it seems to me that the virtue of this liberation I have spoken of is that it leads one on to cherish a vision of life as a whole, not this side or that side only, just as it releases us from the embattled and devouring " ego " which loves to preoccupy and possess us.

Perhaps what I have written, or some of it, may seem fanciful; yet this is what I have experienced from Chinese painting. I recall the first beginnings of my acquaintance with this art, when in the West its existence was hardly suspected; my ignorant, fascinated, eager gropings for fuller knowledge of the new world which it disclosed; the gradual discovery of the masters (due, chiefly, I must record, to the beautiful reproductions published by the Japanese); the moments of supreme pleasure in some exquisite harmony of colour, unknown to Europe, or in the almost throbbing strokes and blots of a master's ink-charged brush. I recall these many years and the gifts they brought me, and I want to express with a whole heart my unending gratitude to the Chinese genius and all that it has meant to the world.

CHINESE ART AND ARCHITECTURE

Selections from the works of
Roger Fry
(with prefatory note by Margery Fry)

THE present century has seen a great widening of the range of our æsthetic appreciation. Perhaps the perfection of photography has brought home to the ordinary person the fact that the plastic arts have other aims than mere representation. It has certainly enabled that ordinary person to grow up in familiarity, at any rate in reproduction, with the works of artists of civilisations remote from our own in time, space, or phase. Such a familiarity is an immense help to understanding : one learns something of the meaning of an unknown art, as of a foreign language, by mere exposure to its influence. It was noticeable at the Chinese Exhibition in London that very few members of the huge popular crowds who streamed through it seemed to be deterred from admiration, as they surely would have been thirty years earlier, simply by the unaccustomedness of the artists' idiom.

No one roamed this wider field of æsthetic experience with more happiness than Roger Fry. After having gained in his earlier years an extended knowledge of the schools of painting and sculpture through which the main tradition of European art has passed, in later life he delighted in finding again the expression of the same fundamental qualities in the work of remoter or more primitive artists, from Sumer or Ordos, from Tel el Amarna or from Benin, from Central America or from Siam.

But it was with paintings, Chinese works of art of certain epochs, that he felt himself most easily and naturally at home : of these he wrote with peculiar pleasure.

Yet, though every artist will have special affinities with some groups of other artists and tend to have a special appreciation of their products, works of art—like people—cannot be rightly loved or understood in the mass. It is a mark of very blunt sensibility or of insincerity to value them because of their school or period. So most of Roger Fry's appreciating and analyses were closely connected with actual examples of the particular master or epoch he was studying, and it is difficult to sever them from context and from illustrations without draining them of all meaning in the process. Nevertheless, I hope that the selections which follow will give to readers unacquainted with his work some idea of what the qualities were which, in his judgment, are the special glories of Chinese art, and what is the magnitude of the debt for the enrichment of our own lives which we of Western civilisations owe to the artists of China.

In making these selections from his writings I am endeavouring to acknowledge on his behalf my brother's own personal share of this debt. I can confidently say that this would have been his own profound desire.

The cross-headings are inserted by me, and are not quotations.

MARGERY FRY.

CHINESE CIVILISATION[1]

Chinese art grew up in a complex and organised social system. This system must be regarded indeed as, in its main outlines, one of the least imperfect social adjustments of the conflicting desires of individuals that have ever been devised, if we may judge from the fact that it has had some kind of continuity of tradition from the third millennium before Christ (and perhaps even from Neolithic times) down to our own day, a record which surpasses that of Egypt itself.

[1] From *The Arts of Painting and Sculpture*. Gollancz, 1932.

THE EUROPEAN CONFRONTED BY CHINESE ART[1]

Almost every work of art comes to us with some letter of introduction or other. There is almost inevitably some intermediary who or which modifies the state of mind with which we approach the interview. If it is a modern work it may be by an artist whom we know and like personally, and at once we are prepared to give it the benefit of every doubt. It may be by an artist whose work has previously bored or irritated us, and the chances are a thousand to one against our giving it a patient hearing. It may come to us with the romantic thrill of intense antiquity, and we feel inclined to make every allowance for a man who took the trouble to live so very long ago and yet to be a quite recognisable human being not altogether unlike ourselves.

It may belong to some exotic civilisation which has already in quite unrelated and accidental ways stirred our imagination, and we are in a hurry to find confirmation of all our past emotions. Or it may be just the contrary, the strangeness, the foreignness of the conceptions may repel us by hinting from the first at what a lot of trouble we should have to take to get sufficiently familiar with the religious or philosophical ideas which we dimly guess at behind the artist's iconography.

[1] From *Transformations*. Chatto & Windus, 1926.

There is no doubt that some of these accessory feelings which cluster round a work of art, like the patina on an ancient bronze, may have a genuine value for our imaginative life, but it is also certain that we cannot make full contact with a work of art, cannot really come to terms of intimacy with its creator, until we have recognised and made allowance for this intervening medium.

When we are considering works of Chinese art this intervening medium tends to distort our vision in various and sometimes contrary directions. There are still, I believe, many people well acquainted with some aspects of European art who yet feel that the art of China is strange to them. They lack a clue to direct them in so unfamiliar a world. They may know but little of Christian hagiology, but at least the names of the Christian Pantheon are familiar to their ears, whereas they have no feelings at all about Avalokatesvaras, Amidhas and Arhats. Again, the whole Chinese symbolism will be unintelligible to them. They know, perhaps, that the dragon is symbolical of the heavens, but they do not feel any point in the symbol, being familiar with dragons only in quite other settings. It may well be that this remoteness of subject-matter in Chinese art makes them feel it is a closed book to them. They may feel happy enough in the presence of the trifling bibelots, the Chinoiseries of later periods, which have become acclimatised in our drawing-rooms, but the great art, above all the early religious art, will repel them by its strangeness.

Now, I believe this is a mistaken fear. Chinese art is in reality extremely accessible to the European sensibility, if one approaches it in the same mood of attentive passivity which we cultivate before an Italian masterpiece of the Renaissance, or a Gothic or Romanesque sculpture. A man need not be a Sinologist to understand the æsthetic appeal of a Chinese statue. It may represent some outlandish divinity, but it is expressed according to certain principles of design and by means of a definite rhythm. And it so happens that both the principles of Chinese design and the nature of their rhythms are not half so unfamiliar to the European eye as Chinese musical rhythms are to our ears. On the contrary, they are so similar that I could point to certain much-loved European artists who are nearer in this respect to the Chinese than they are to certain other great European artists. Chinese art is nothing like so difficult of access as Hindu art. It has, to begin with, colour schemes that are pre-eminently harmonious to the European eye ; it has the same general notions of logical and clear co-ordination of the parts within the whole ; it aims at a similar equilibrium, and it does not allow the elaboration of detail to destroy the general structure.

ÆSTHETIC FREEDOM OF CHINESE ARTISTS[1]

We have seen that for the most part art of
the ancient empires was controlled by its non-
æsthetic social functions ; that imposing scale
and perfection of finish were aimed at, and that
only here and there could the artist express even
tentatively his individual sensibility. China is
the only great, early, highly organised civilisation
in which we feel that the artist's sensibility comes
fully into play. When we look at the bronzes
of the Chou period, we feel that however rigidly
the artist may have been bound to observe
certain rules in order to conform to the principles
of magic and ritual, within these limits he had
freedom. Each one of these vessels appears as
a new discovery of plastic harmonies of the
most surprising kind. The proportions of each
part with regard to the whole, the exact curve
of the galb, or profile, the projection of the
moulded ornamentation, all have been felt with
an intense imaginative conviction. Moreover,
however marvellous the technical skill required
for such elaborate metal work, this is never
insisted on, nothing is sacrificed to mere finish ;
the idea of luxury is absent. Chou bronzes are
in fact for the most part pure works of art.
Moreover, wherever animal forms enter into
the design, as they often do, we notice that the

[1] *The Arts of Painting and Sculpture.* Gollancz, 1932.

C

Chinese artist has retained, perhaps from more primitive times, that peculiar instinctive grasp of vital rhythm which seems so often to disappear from a civilised and self-conscious art. The little that is left to us of true sculpture—mostly animal forms—bears out what is said above, and these remain indeed among the most perfect works of their kind that we know of.

WATER-COLOUR AND HANDWRITING[1]

A stroke of opaque oil paint upon a canvas gives to the eye a single positive statement of a particular tone and colour, there is nothing uncertain about it ; but a wash of water-colour on silk is varied at every point by the different thicknesses of liquid which have dried or been absorbed by the silk at various points. It does not make any one positive statement, but suggests the possibility of different interpretations. The painter in oil is committed, by the positive statement contained in his first brush stroke, to complete the texture of his image by covering his canvas. The water-colourist, particularly if working on silk, can leave large surfaces of untouched silk between the various parts of the total vision to which he wishes to call our attention.

.   .   .   .   .

[1] *The Arts of Painting and Sculpture.* Gollancz, 1932.

Oil paint, having a certain viscosity, tends to cause a drag on the artist's gesture in making a touch, whilst liquid water-colour leaves the gesture nearly free. The result is that what is called, by analogy, the " handwriting " of Chinese pictures is more clearly evident than it is in most European painting. This handwriting, which records the habitual and dominant unconscious reactions of the artist, supplies one of the most direct expressions of his sensibility. In his main design an artist expresses his deliberately chosen and conscious rhythmic idea ; in his handwriting he carries this out with innumerable subtle inflections and variations which, in the case of a felicitous choice of idea, harmonise with and enrich the main theme. Great as the importance of " handwriting " always has been and must be, in the art of painting, it has nowhere been recognised as clearly and exploited as deliberately as by Chinese artists. Indeed their appreciation of linear rhythm has led them to regard calligraphy (handwriting in its literal sense) as one of the fine arts. A fine specimen of the handwriting of a master is treasured as much as a masterpiece of painting, and this attitude has constantly reacted in turn upon painting itself. This keen appreciation of handwriting has not been without its dangers to Chinese art, . . . and its effects would have been greater had not Chinese artists and writers on art insisted from early times

(fifth century A.D.) on the need for the rhythm to
conform to the vital rhythms of living things.

.   .   .   .   .

With comparatively rare exceptions, Chinese art
seems to have been the direct outcome of æsthetic
impulses aiming at pure spiritual satisfactions.
A certain proportion of the minor works of art
bear the impress of the desire for luxury and have
the inexpressive shop-finish which results from
that, but in the main art was not captured by
society for biological ends. It was a free art.
The Chinese are perhaps the only people who have
constantly recognised the spiritual function of
art in a way that has only happened occasionally
elsewhere.[1]

CHINESE LANDSCAPES

The Chinese feeling for landscape and particularly for what we call romantic landscape, mountains and torrents, has been well analysed by
Mr. Waley. He shows how, with the over-
elaborate machinery of the Chinese bureaucracy—
a bureaucracy, moreover, composed of the most
highly educated and cultured men of all classes—
the desire to escape from the pressure of social
life became a frequent obsession of more sensitive
natures. They longed to live the life of the

[1] Chinese artists never painted their pictures to be
sold.—ED.

hermit, " to live free and fearless in the isolation of the hills." This impulse had nothing of the ascetic-religious impulse which drove the early Christians into the Thebaid. It was rather the ideal of complete self-realisation by release from social pressure. Those, too, who never even attempted this flight from society, adored " mountains and torrents as symbols of escape," and for them landscape paintings, in which this aspect of nature was emphasised, became a source of spiritual satisfaction.

CHINESE IMPRESSIONISM[1]
(Notes on an eleventh-century copy of a ninth-century picture)

That there was a great school of landscape painting as early as the T'ang dynasty there can be no doubt, but nothing of it remains. This is a Sung copy after Wang Wei, the greatest landscapist of T'ang times—but it clearly shows more the feeling of Sung than of T'ang times in the delicacy and fragility of its forms. It is strange to think that in the eleventh or twelfth centuries Chinese civilisation had reached such a point as this—could give to individuals that detachment from the ordinary concerns of life that would enable them to indulge in such a sophisticated response

[1] From Roger Fry's Slade Lectures to be published shortly by the Cambridge University Press.

to natural appearance as this. Only people who sought their pleasures in contemplation rather than action could arrive at such a deep understanding of the spiritual overtones of natural appearances as this artist has expressed.

It is a very curious fact that the Chinese who disregarded the obvious effect of light and shade in their rendering of persons and objects should have been thus sensitive to the far subtler tone relations by which we express such atmospheric effects—and should in this direction have anticipated Western art by nearly one thousand years. Nothing quite like this can be seen in Europe before the later nineteenth century. Rubens is the only artist of earlier times who noted and expressed those moments when the familiar forms of the landscape are veiled and transmuted by the mists of sunrise or twilight—but his robust and straightforward nature was incapable of the remote elusiveness and the subtle implications of such a work as this. Perhaps Seurat gives us our nearest European parallel and he, too, like this T'ang artist, relied mainly for his expression upon the feeling for intervals.

ANIMAL, MONSTER, AND MAN IN CHINESE ART[1]

Probably the imaginative sympathy with the inner life of animals is a phase of all early human

[1] From *Transformations*. Chatto & Windus, 1926.

life ; but, generally, it seems to have disappeared before men reached the full self-consciousness of civilisation. In China, on the other hand, the civilised consciousness seems to supervene so early that it does not destroy this primeval understanding with the animal world. These Chinese artists, even the earliest of them, are people more or less of our own kind. They are already fully conscious artists ; they speak a language of form which presents no barrier to us. The objects which they created seem to be as clearly made for the leisured contemplation, the purely æsthetic enjoyment, which we ourselves give to them, as the works of, say, the Italian Renaissance. We need not fear that they are happy accidents, the unintentional by-products of some other activity. We feel that we share the artist's own delight, that we can establish a communion with his spirit. He reports to us in our own language that dim sense of continuity with nature, the memory of which was lost so long ago by our own ancestors.

In China, that spirit of detachment from the human point of view which enabled the primitive comprehension of non-human life to survive, persists under civilised conditions. The sentiment of intimacy and kinship with animals naturally grows less as the primitive feeling is at last forgotten. Here and there, from the Sung dynasty onwards, we find it replaced by a purely picturesque and external curiosity such as modern

European art habitually displays. But even as late as Ming times an echo of that earlier sympathy with animal life occasionally survives.

Not altogether unconnected with this attitude to animals, and at least as strange to the Western mind, is the absence in Chinese art of the Tragic spirit. Whilst their fun is sometimes almost childishly naïve and exuberant, their gravity is never altogether untouched by humour. A Michelangelo is unthinkable in the atmosphere of Chinese art; still more, perhaps, an El Greco, letting himself go whithersoever the exaltation of his fevered imagination carried him. This kind of exaltation, this dramatic intensity of human feeling, seems unknown to the Chinese. Their most exalted religious feeling leads them into a more contemplative mood, one more remote from possible action than ours. It is a mood, too, which admits of a certain playful humour which we are not accustomed to associate with such states of mind.

These characteristics are connected, no doubt, with that happy disinterestedness of which I have spoken. It, too, is the reward of not having fallen into the habit of human arrogance. Since, the Chinese might argue, the world does not revolve round us as its centre, we need not take either the world or ourselves too seriously. We can afford to play. We can play with the offspring of our imagination. They shall be our playthings and our delight. We need not take even them too seriously. If we like to imagine monsters we will, but however real we make them, we need not be frightened by them. They are only being terrible in play. And so it comes about that however portentous Chinese monsters may be, they are never tragic, like the progeny of our mediæval fancies. The mediæval mind frightened itself by its own activity. No one could apply the word " Dantesque " to a Chinese creation.

INFLUENCE OF THE CHINESE ART ON THE WEST[1]

The Greek who fixed the chains of anthropo-centrism upon us gave us none the less its antidote in science, and modern science has perhaps, by its repeated blows at our arrogant assumptions, at last prepared the Western mind to accept the freedom and gaiety of the Chinese attitude. The influence of Chinese art seems to be continually increasing in the West, and nothing could be more fruitful to our art than to absorb something of the spirit—though it is to be hoped we shall not copy the forms—which inspires the great examples.

Chinese art appealed to Western nations origin-ally almost entirely in virtue of its technical ingenuity, its brilliant and tasteful execution, and

[1] From *Transformations*. Chatto & Windus, 1926.

the " quaintness " due to its unfamiliarity. As
we get to know it better, as we explore more and
more the great classic periods, we are led to treat
it with the same respect and the same concentrated
attention which we have to devote to our own
great masters if we would apprehend the nature
of their states of mind.

CHINA AND THE WEST COMPARED

We need not be surprised that Chinese literature, so far as we can get at it through translations, and Chinese art offer relatively few
obstacles to our apprehension. . . . I should
like to begin by emphasising this fundamental
similarity. Of course, our European civilisation
has not been consistently tinged with rational-
ism, we have had our periods of unreason, but in
those ages such as the centuries of Graeco-Roman
civilisation and Renaissance and post-Renaissance
Europe it has been distinctly rationalist, and
curiously enough (it may be a mere accident or
it may not), during those ages our architecture
has been mainly what we call classic. I don't
want to go into the meaning of this word, I
use it merely as a convenient label for a particular
type of architecture in which the main elements
of structure are given with sufficient simplicity
to enable us to relate the parts easily—are not
too much overlaid or obscured—at least an

architecture in which rectilinear forms pre-dominate. It is true that Chinese wooden pavilions, with their great protruding and upturned roofs, do strike us as odd, fantastic, and exotic, and indeed these forms have so seized on the European imagination that they have become symbols of the Chinese style, none the less if you look at photographs of the ordinary country-side, at farmhouses, bridges, gateways, and so on, they are so familiar that one might suppose them to be in Italy or the South of France. For the most part the architecture of the great periods of Chinese art has been destroyed in the course of her terribly catastrophic history, but if we look at the few ancient buildings that are left we feel at once that it belongs to our classic tradition. Though the cornices are carried out further than Italian architects would have done we instantly understand the main idea and accept without difficulty the choice of proportions.

. . . . . .

I wanted from the first to posit this classical element in Chinese art because to such an extent the popular notion of Chinese art has been derived from exceptional periods—periods when the Chinese were enjoying a Rococo in digression from the classical period—just as Europe did in the eighteenth century.

THE VILLAGE AND ITS SCHOLAR

E. R. Hughes

I HAVE a picture in my study, some five feet
long and eighteen inches from top to bottom.
It is a landscape—in black and white, as our expression goes, but actually showing all shades of
lovely grey. The foreground is in the right-hand
corner, the background away to the left, a painting analysable into five sections, yet essentially a
unity : mountains and their mists, pines, bamboos, a river promontory, flats of sand, all part
of the one theme, a river winding its way out of
the hill country to the plain. I have watched such
scenes scores of time as my boat swung creaking
down-stream with its cargo of bamboo paper or
dried mushrooms, and maybe a huge coffin
built of long-seasoned timber and destined for
some rich merchant in a coast port. The artist
gives it all back to me, in spring as he saw it, but
also in summer and autumn and winter.

This is the window I have on my inside wall.
Through it I look away into China. Here in the
foreground is the farm my boat is just passing,
just beyond the farm the sturdy plank bridge by

which the farmer and his family get to their fields, over there the path which winds to the ferry, the farmer's short cut to market. This is China, China of the peasants as they have fitted their lives to the rhythm of the seasons, have dug and manured and harrowed and again dug and manured and harrowed for at least two thousand years. I am thinking more of the south, and so say " two thousand years." Of the north I should have to say three thousand and more years, for it was in the Yellow River basin that Chinese civilisation had its rise and then took wings to itself. It found wings of the spirit, and by the time that Greece was creating our spiritual heritage China was creating hers in art and poetry and philosophy.

Courts and their capitals figure in that culture, but not to the extent that many have supposed. The earliest thinkers in China had so deep an appreciation of agriculture as the root and all other industries as the branches of a people's life : they lent such a dignity to the farmer's toil and so linked it to their sense of a numinous authority in nature that their people have never been able to forget their words. China's civilisation and culture, therefore, is a rural one at heart, not an urban one, and we have to look in the country for the influences which made it a culture at all. A peasantry which has to wrestle with hard economic conditions, as the Chinese have for the most part had to wrestle, does not easily avoid the temptation to bucolic lethargy of spirit and dumb subservience. Even the greatest of prophetic utterances by teachers of sacred memory do not come near to the farmer. There must be somebody alongside the peasant who can help him to see his toiling life as placed in a setting which is imbued with noble issues. For this reason we have to turn our attention to the "village scholar." Only so can we understand the spiritual strength of China with its age-old co-operation of the peasant and the scholar: the scholar who, if he did not live in the same house, at any rate lived next door.

To go back to classical times, we find evidence of the village scholar in the third century B.C. The old literati affirmed that he existed considerably earlier, and they cited the Classic of Rites as proof. If we are to believe certain passages there, the great King Wen and his equally great son, Chou Kung, organised education both in the Chou capital and in the capitals of the feudal states, and thereafter there came to be schools in all the villages as well as the district centres. Unfortunately the evidence against is too strong for any such belief to be possible. All we can say is that at the end of the sixth century Confucius was the first of a long succession of philosopher-teachers of all sorts of schools of thought, that they welcomed as disciples men of plebeian as

well as patrician family, and that so there came to
be a class of wandering scholars, going from
court to court and primed with advice on how to
save the country. For the more honest of these
the times were unpropitious, and there is good
reason for assuming that by the end of the fourth
century a number of them were settled in their
ancestral homes and teaching young boys as well
as young men. In mid-third-century literature
we find the two following passages.

One is from a series of four sections on education and its advantages, and whilst the first two
sections might well apply only to the education of
young patricians, the last can almost be described
as a tract advocating universal education. The
third is of special interest because it describes
in lively fashion the defects of a bad teacher and
the unhappy consequences for his disciples
(*ti tzŭ*). " They are uncomfortable while they are
living with their teachers, and when they come
home they are in disgrace with their parents and
brothers whilst outside the family they are
ashamed before their well-educated friends both
in town and village." There is a ring of truth
about that passage. It is not the work of a
Utopian dreamer who pictured a golden age long
ago in which sage emperors established school
houses in every village.

The other passage comes in a book by the
scion of a ducal house. He loathed all the talk

he heard from the Confucians and Mohists about love and justice and holding up noble examples to the people to be good. To him it was the very mockery of government, and he would not even believe that parents loved their children for anything more than their own selfish ends. And in any case, he said, love was not the way to make a good member of society. He illustrated this. " Here is a bad son. His parents are displeased with him, but he does not reform, the people of the village reprove him, but he does not budge from his ways, his teacher explains how he ought to act, but he does not change. The love of his parents, the actions of the neighbours, the wisdom of his teacher, three noble influences added together, and in the end he will not budge. Not a hair of his shin-bone [lit.] is reformed. But let the official from the district centre only come with his officers and soldiers, bent on the law being put into effect and looking for rebellious men, then the bad son is afraid and all of a tremble. He changes all his ways. Thus we see parents' love is not enough to lead their sons in the way they should go. It has to wait for the official and his severe punishments." We may assume, I think, that in the third century B.C. there were some villages which had scholars living in them, teaching those who wished to learn, and not finding that all their disciples were as bad as Han Fei made out.

Forty years later we find them in a different rôle, stirring the peasants to revolt against the tyrannical rule of Ch'in. By the middle of the second century there was peace and prosperity under the Han Emperors, Wen Ti and Ching Ti, and with these conditions came a revival of learning. It was then probably that the legends about the sage emperors and their schools took concrete shape : that was the way in which the people who believed in the extension of education commended their ideas to the Court and its Grand Officers. It is certain that there was a movement throughout the country in this direction, for a number of passages in Pan Ku's *History of the Han Dynasty* point to this. The account of the man who brought Szechuan in the far west within the p ale of civilisation is very clear on this, the move to popularise education, whilst Liu Hsin's famous index of extant literature which Pan Ku used contains a description of how the village schoolmasters taught writing.

In the second decade of the first century B.C. we have from another source excellent evidence of the power of the country scholar being recognised by the Court. Times were bad, the country exhausted by Wu Ti's vast imperialistic schemes, and the economy of the country worsened rather than improved by the Government's monopoly of salt and iron and its practice of buying grain when prices were down and

D

selling it when they were up. The reason they gave for this practice was that so they could stabilise prices and stop the big merchant operators from fleecing the community. Actually the system led to continual abuse, whilst the monopoly in iron led to the farmer being put to great inconvenience in getting his implements ; when he did get them they were badly made. It was at this time that the country scholars made themselves heard, and the result was that sixty of them were summoned to the capital to put the farmers' case before the authorities. According to Huan K'uan's account some years later—a very spirited account in the form of a debate— the scholars showed themselves sensible, well-informed representatives of the farmer's interests. At the same time they solemnly affirmed the great Confucian principles of government being rooted in the moral power of the governors and justifying itself only by bringing prosperity to the common man as well as to those who served the community in higher ways.

It was this moral basis to social life which made the heart of education, whether in the aristocratic school or college in the capital or in the simple country establishment where one teacher did the best he could. Of the " three Rs " arithmetic did not take much of the disciple's time, but writing took more. By the second century A.D. calligraphy was well on its way to becoming the most poetic and dynamic of all the arts. Composition also was a serious business. Some of the best Chinese prose was written during Han times as well as some of the worst, whilst verse-making, either in the austere northern style or the romantic southern, had its insistent appeal. But the main task of the teacher was to make his disciples able to read, able to understand and appreciate the moral grandeur and authority of the accepted writings. That was on the intellectual side. There was another side, a training in ritual, part religious, part social, and exercises in music and dancing and archery and chariot driving. We may doubt whether the latter ever took much hold in the primitive schools in the country : they were for the young men in Court circles, as also was familiarisation with the great imperial rituals. But it was during this era that the old rituals of ancestor worship and family life were adapted and exalted so that they became the actual poetic expression of the common man's life. The daily round and common task of man or woman was set to a noble tune, and although for most of them there was no education in letters, there was very much an education in ritual. This was where the village scholar made himself most deeply felt, for he was the expert in these great matters. He could also point to the passages in the sacred books where it was laid down that the pattern of the State was the

pattern of the family and it was only when the
family virtues were practised by all classes in
society from the Emperor to his meanest subject
that the blessing of Heaven descended.

Those sixty country scholars in the pages of
Huan K'uan's book are immensely significant.
The Chief Secretary, with whom they argued,
paid the barest lip-service to Confucian principles. His attitude quite plainly was the Legalist
one, the realist attitude as we call it to-day, concerned only with the factors making for political
power. We have to assume to-day, as traditional
scholarship never could, that there was a large
admixture of this spirit in Chinese statesmanship ;
and by this assumption we come to see the power
of the Confucianism which had laid hold of the
minds of the people. No emperor could afford
to leave it out of account, because the farmers and
the artisans and the merchants had come to believe
in what their scholar uncles and brothers had
told them was the truth.

The history of China from the third century on
to the seventh is a particularly fascinating study
for Europeans. At the same time that the Roman
Empire was breaking up and the West came so
near to losing the civilisation it prized, the
Chinese were subject to the same grinding test of
internal schism and invasion by barbarian tribes.
In both hemispheres the old culture proved itself
adequate to survive. The very chieftains who

were so contemptuous of civilised ways became converts to them and ranged themselves as defenders of the faith. As for religion, two new faiths which recognised no racial divisions came in this era of confusion to be strong bulwarks for the spirits of hard-driven men and women : in Western Europe Christianity, in Eastern Asia Buddhism.

The parallel, however, must not be pressed too far. Whereas in Europe the old pagan faiths went down, in China they did not. Religious Taoism alongside of philosophic Taoism survived, whilst Confucianism—not to be confounded with primitive paganism—retained its influence in spite of the exotic attractions of foreign cults. Not only so : in Western Europe the unity for which Rome stood was broken into pieces in spite of Charlemagne's resounding achievement. The peoples came to be divided among a mass of warring feudal states. That was not the outcome in China. The T'ang Emperors (620–907) ruled a China which had a new and richer unity, and the same applies to the Sung Emperors (960–1280) in whose time Confucianism reformed itself, drawing from philosophic Buddhism and Taoism a new power of intellectual subtlety.

The question is how this great force of cultural and political unity came to be there. Who were the persons—for in the last resort it must be persons—whose influence told in this striking fashion among the tens of millions of the inhabitants of those great areas ? One has to be careful, of course, in dealing with such wide tracts of history which have been so little subjected to the scrutiny of impartial minds ; but we are driven back to the simple historical phenomenon that in spite of cruel wars and Nature calamities life did continue. The farmer produced the necessary food-stuffs, and along with the continuance of physical life there was also a continuance of spiritual tradition. We can go further than this and consider the predilection that sophisticated Courts have for bizarre foreign cults. Individual emperors might be attracted, some were very greatly attracted by Buddhism and spent time and money prodigally in the practice of their new religion. But the civil service examinations went on as before, and the servants of the State were steeped in the old books. The old sacrifices had to be carried out : the old altars and temples were there, built on the pattern of heaven and earth and the order of the seasons. If these sacramental rites should be abandoned, the news would spread throughout the country, and although the fears of the silly farmers might be ignored, the stern disapproval of the scholars by their side was another matter. So on the wide scale of history extending over centuries of peace alternating with confusion, it was in those innumerable villages spread through the great rural areas that the will for unity persisted. The peasants by themselves could never have achieved such a will, for the peasant's horizon is inevitably circumscribed. But with the scholar to help him it could be done, particularly when the scholar saw government as a religious act based on the community of life in the common soil and harmonising all men within the four seas.

There is a famous line, *su i wei hsüan hsi*, in an old old poem which has not otherwise survived : " the plain ground for the colours." That is what we have to look for in that vast colourful tapestry which is Chinese history. In weaving there could be no fabric if there were not the warp with its sober colouring mixing in with the brilliant colours of the weft. To change the metaphor back to painting, the scholar and peasant in the village are " the plain ground." As such they are unknown to history. And yet, if we get close to the former, as we can do through all sorts of literary remains, we find the plain ground by no means so plain as we begin by supposing. Take the *Dictionary of National Biography* (published ten years ago) with its thumb-nail sketches of nearly forty thousand individuals more or less known to fame ; among them, on every page, there are some who are recorded as coming from the country and going back to the country to live out their honoured old age. Take the local gazetteers for the making of which the Chinese have had a passion for hundreds of years, and in which are to be found the deeds and the publications of the local worthies. Take also the prefaces to the innumerable editions of worth-while books, and the prefaces to the collected works of this poetaster and that essay-writer. And then explore the provincial histories with an eye for the special characteristics of the people of Hunan, for example, as against the people of Kiangsi next door to them, the people of Kwantung as against their neighbours of Kwangsi or Fukien. This " plain ground " becomes rich with variety and incident. A rural civilisation, and conservative as all rural civilisations are, but not hidebound, not cut to a monotonous pattern or impervious to new ideas. We have only to turn to the histories of developments in thought, in painting and ceramics, in poetry, and in novel writing and dramatics, to be convinced that things might move slowly, but they did move. Even in so reactionary an era as the Ming the Jesuit Fathers found keen minds ready to absorb their knowledge of physical science, whilst they and the Franciscans before them made converts in most of the eighteen provinces. One turns to the dictum of a modern historian, " of all that human misery which prevails in the vast spaces of Asia, Africa, and

South America, where thousands of millions of men and women have lived, worked, and died, leaving no memorial, contributing nothing to the future." Whatever the truth may be about Africa and South America, his words are the very reverse of the truth about the hundreds of millions who in succeeding ages have composed the State and nation of China. In their villages and towns, even more than their imperial capitals and provincial centres, they have contributed a manner of life which, near as it was to the soil and the harsh exigencies of the economic struggle, was yet able to produce an exquisite refinement of manners, an appreciation of beauty in nature, and alongside this, indeed as the root of it, a consistent exaltation of family harmony and of the universe as a moral order.

The argument of this enquiry has broken out of the historical mould in which it started, and the last paragraph has without warning brought the reader down to later ages, the Ming and the Manchu eras, without a reference to the Mongol period. It was inevitable that it should be so with so vast a subject. But this enables us to turn our attention in conclusion to modern times, to what living observers have seen with their own eyes. Perhaps as one of these—for I lived for nearly twenty years in the interior of South China—I may intrude my own experience. I have known dozens of country scholars, been acquainted with hundreds : so also with the farmers, for you could not know the one without coming to know the other. The time was a bad one for nearly all of them, those early years of the Republic which produced the war-lord regime and in so many districts came near to breaking up the age-old fabric of village life. For the old-fashioned literatus the situation easily became rather tragic. For one thing the last decades of the Manchu rule had been such as to sow grievous doubts in men's minds. Was this majestic system of learning to which they pinned their faith as important as they thought it ? Did it, indeed, fit in at all with this modern world with which, whether she liked it or not, their China must come to terms ? The doubts went very deep, and the village scholar lost confidence in himself.

True as this is, yet it is not the whole truth, nor even the most significant part of the truth. I saw these men adapting themselves to meet the new conditions ; and I saw the peasants standing by their leaders and teachers. Who else was there to whom they could look for guidance ? I saw also the new scholars, the products of the new schools, taking on the duties which their fathers and uncles handed on to them and adding on to these new duties which emerged. There were times when I wondered whether they could ever be as good as the men who had served before them ; they had not the same sense of an authoritative tradition. But on the whole the striking thing was that such a big majority of them should carry on as they did with the old principles applied as best might be. This, after all, is not to be wondered at. The family continued and parents were parents and sons and daughters-in-law still sons and daughters-in-law. In spite of all sorts of changes due to Western ideas of individual self-fulfilment, the intricate nexus of family economy had to be preserved, the old rituals of family courtesy were too precious to be discarded. So long as the land could be worked and the rice bowls more or less filled, so long as communications were open and markets could be held, with all that that meant for local craftsmen and shopkeepers, so long as education continued and there was a chance for the clever boy to get out in the world and be a credit and a profit to his ancestral village, just for so long there was every inducement to progressives and conservatives to co-operate in holding the place together. In how many villages I saw, during the worst years of the Republic, new school-houses erected, with their characteristic woodwork painted a bright blue. The villages were not rich, indeed according to Western standards they were markedly poor, but the young graduates of the district high school, together with some of the old scholars, wanted the job of teaching and the money for it; and since the place must have a school, it might as well show the other villages that it knew how to run one properly. So the subscription list would go round and the money or the labour or the materials would be forthcoming. And how many times I have gone in and seen the teaching in progress, seen also farmers lounging there, as they watched what was going on in *their* school with *their* young sons and brothers and cousins being started on the road to learning and culture (*hsiao wen*).

My face-to-face experience of Chinese village life is limited to the south, where economic conditions are better and have been so for hundreds of years. I do not know at first hand the rural areas in the north which have been inundated with floods or stricken with complete crop failure. But what I have seen of minor calamities and the scourge of the lesser war-lords leads me to the belief that although there are limits clearly to the blows which this village life can sustain, yet given any sort of grounds for hope in the future, the community persists; and it persists not merely as an economic order, but also as a spiritual order built on its old foundations.

The Communist Party in China has maintained the opposite. Its cry is that the abuses in the present system—whether old or new makes no difference—are so fundamental and ineradicable that nothing but reorganisation from top to bottom can make village life possible. Wherever the Red Armies have been in control they claim to have done this with success and the approval of the peasants. In so far as their policy has been agrarian, ensuring for the farmer the fruits of his toil and saving him from villainous taxation, this claim must be allowed. But there is nothing to show that the pure Communist programme appeals to the peasant, and there is plenty of evidence that he hates revolutionary interference with the spirit of the family. He will compromise with the people of his own clan and neighbourhood and hammer out in endless talk the plans of reform on which agreement can be reached ; but so long as he is on the land of his fathers, he refuses to be dragooned by outside authorities into economic or any other kind of mechanical efficiency. He is in fact in his own way an individualist with the individualism of the man whose principles are instinctive and not reasoned. He just knows that the solution of any problem must be a human one, and that means that the natural human duties as well as the natural human desires must be taken into account. It is here that bureaucratically minded and ideologically minded officials break down with their impatient desire for quick results. They fail to get co-operation, the co-operation which the old scholar got because he took time to explain what a man or a woman ought to do and allowed for time in which they could come to see it for themselves.

My space has gone, and there has been no description of the multifarious duties which fell to the lot of the village scholar. A brief paragraph must suffice. Much depended, of course, on the temperament of a man. If he was a pure scholar immersed in his scholarship, his family and neighbours would tend to leave him to his own pursuits, the more so because he could not be expected to show a practical mind in mundane affairs. Even so the village was proud of his other-worldliness and acknowledged his spiritual authority in times of crisis, just as in an English village everyone reverenced the saintly scholar parson. But in the general run of cases the scholar was expected to see to it that education was available for the young. Also he had to do his duty as an elder. That meant a knowledge of village affairs such as the care of roads and bridges. Perhaps the chief function of all was in being ready to arbitrate along with other men of standing in the disputes and personal quarrels which were always liable to break out. The official court of the *hsien chang* (county head) was there as a last resort, but the better mind of the Chinese people has always been to refer a matter to voluntary arbitration with one's own people who know the circumstances. They only can point out a real basis of moral agreement. A function of this kind could, if a scholar was wise in human nature, take up a large part of his time : time for which he was duly paid in meals and money. And then there were all the other small matters, the writing of letters for those who could not do it themselves, the superintending of marriage arrangements, the drawing up of the rightly worded notice of a death in the family, the drawing of land deeds and deeds of partnership in a business venture. There was no end to what a man might be called on to do, and given that he and his fellows were both intelligent and public-spirited, they made all the difference to the peace and prosperity of the community as a whole. The proviso must be taken seriously. The peasant's reverence for learning was not merely because of learning's practical usefulness, but also because of the moral power it gave. And this reverence persisted in spite of bitter experience at the hands of scholar drones and scholar sharks, the whole tribe of rack-renting landlords, usurious money-lenders, and " running dogs," the men who nosed their way into people's affairs in order to make profit for themselves. Every country-side knew these to their cost just as they knew the others who made life good.

In the early days of the Republic there was a certain village scholar in a mountain valley in the

far west of Fukien Province. He had read much
of Western ways, though he had never been
to the coast to see what was being done in those
new Treaty Ports. He saw the necessity of de-
vising new methods for building up the economy
of his clan and village. He sent his eldest son to
Foochow to learn the new education, and had
some of the young men trained in more skilled
processes of weaving. Then came the Revolution, and he listened to all that was said about
liberty and democracy. Some of it appealed to
him, some of it did not. After weighing things
up in his mind he decided, without consulting
anyone, what he would do. He gut up early one
morning, went down to the ancestral temple,
and there on the front wall, with his big-character
brush, he wrote in large letters what he thought
needed saying : " The liberty of the people is
the liberty of honouring the law." Twelve years
later I was in that village and saw this sentence
on the wall. His teacher-son told me the story
of it, and that night, after entertaining me, the
leaders of the three clans meeting in that temple
which was also a school, told me how the influence
of the old scholar had worked and how they held
the place together in the bad times they were
going through. There were the new type of
scholar and the old about me, farmers and weavers
and the blacksmith, with women of all ages on the
outskirts of the group. Behind the altar gleamed

the gold lettering of their ancestors' names on the spirit tablets. The newest among them gleamed the brightest, the name of the man who believed in liberty and saw in it a liberty to obey the law.

LI PO THE POET

Innes Jackson

IT was a warm morning of thick cloud in early
June when I set out from Nanking with
three companions, whom I shall call, in the
modern style, Mr. Wu, Mr. Kao, and Mr. Hsieh ;
and we were to visit the temple of Li Po, a
patriarch of Chinese poetry, on the Promontory
of Rainbow-Coloured Rocks. The three gentle-
men came in Chinese gowns, long, light blue,
and of silk for spring ; Mr. Wu carried a fan,
with poems on it and the bright and splendid
painting of a kingfisher.

The Chinese are friendly people, kind from the
heart, and apparently never happier than when
sharing their goods with others they know to be
appreciative. They will give away their favourite
books to a friend ; they will plan the most
elaborate and careful entertainment ; they will
exercise all their ingenuity to bring pleasure.
This excursion was enchanting from end to
end, and most thoughtfully designed for my
diversion.

We travelled with bags of food : oranges,

gherkins, leechees, bread, tea-leaves, dried and peppered fish, a tin of meat lumps swimming in juice—these were a few of our provisions. In the best of tempers, we caught a local train, passed the time in tea-drinking and, to my great delight, in singing nearly all the way.

It was midday and hot by the time we reached the famous headland, for the clouds had lifted a little, and we could have spasmodic glances of the Yangtze River, the "River of Ten Thousand *Li*," relieved of its turgid colouring and sparkling gallantly. We climbed up from the level by a winding path ; we exclaimed with admiration and quoted to the point. There were few birds here except the large blue and white magpies that flopped on to their feet so lumpishly it was hard to admire them much. One or two bright red creeping wild flowers startled the eye, and down the headland-side poured a pine wood, a streak of the darkest possible green. Some white-sailed fishing boats lay in the river, hardly moving in that oppressive atmosphere.

Li Po the poet was also a fisher of sorts. In a mood of mischief and bitter irony he once visited a Prime Minister known for his corruption, and presented his visiting-card engraved "Li Po, the sea-monster angler."

" What sort of line and hook do you use ? " enquired the Prime Minister pleasantly.

" Opening my heart to the wind and waves,

and my will to the universe, I use the rainbow for line and the bright moon for a hook," said Li.

" What about your bait, old man ? " pursued the Prime Minister, humouring as he thought the poor eccentric.

" A scoundrel ! " thundered Li.

The recorder of the story added that the Prime Minister felt blue at this remark.

In life Li Po was absolutely fearless ; friend of heroes, diplomats, courtiers, the Emperor, he would denounce knavery in the highest places with magnificent cynicism. Yet he was also the most compassionate of men. Before his Court days he lived some years with a hermit in the mountains, to feed thousands of wild birds. Later, at Yangchow, he gave away over three hundred thousand pieces of silver to the poor, and early dispensed with his property to them— as lavish, carefree, and robust as autumn winds. But let no one conjure up a Chinese Saint Francis ; native artists drew him jolly and pot-bellied—a splendid mountain of flesh, and posterity remembers him almost as much for his tipsiness as for his transcendant, unearthly poetry. A tradition says he met death inspired by wine and a poetic impulse to clasp the moon in his arms, as he sailed a boat beneath the Promontory of Rainbow-Coloured Rocks, in a robe given him by the Emperor. There was a moon in the sky and a moon in the water—prodigality of bliss ! The

river seemed more accessible than Heaven, but
the consummation was both cold and sad.

After an hour's amiable meandering we
reached the temple. It seemed well-garnered and
prosperous, and while it served for inn and
restaurant, the pilgrim could also say his prayers
and burn a stick of incense there. I am not sure
whether the act was made in simple veneration—
a supplication for the poet's comfort in another
world—or whether Li Po, by his astonishing
poetic gift, was seriously believed to have joined
the Immortals and to be now, like the starry
Augustus, capable of interceding for common
men.

With so pleasantly Rabelaisian a history, Li's
memorial temple brought no shock of surprise.
At the rear of the shrine sat a life-size image of the
gentleman, dressed in gold and scarlet, hung with
flowers and jewels, and with a smooth painted
face and artificial black whiskers, no more
dignified than a doll.

At the back courtyard we found a large pome-
granate tree, completely covered with its rich
sharp-orange flowers. A few strides from the
shrine was a verandah from which we could watch
the river's eddying and the hills behind it, and
eat our delicacies and others cooked by the
servants. They brought us a bowl full of steam-
ing rice, a dish of young peas, and a river fish
grilled with sugar and ginger and other indeter-

minate but delicious concoctions. They brought
us pots of local wine—cooler, sweeter and paler
than the usual vintage. In our secular way we
honoured the bard, and after, since the afternoon
was as heavy as our eyelids, draped ourselves in
reasonable comfort over the verandah railings
and dozed.

> *" In the cloud-drift her skirt, in the flowers her face ;*
> *Spring wind sweeps the railings, the dew clings thickly.*
> *On the mountain peak of Many Jewels I may see her,*
> *Or meet under moonlight on the Terrace of Jasper. . ."*

This is a poem Li wrote by Royal command.
The Emperor Hsuan Tsung, walking in the
Palace Garden at Ch'ang An with his favourite
mistress, Yang Kuei-Fei, at the time when
peonies were in flower, demanded poems from
Li fit for his happy mood and the Lady Yang's
loveliness. That combination of poetry, peonies,
and passion cost the Emperor his kingdom. He
saw his ambitious mistress's blood drip into
the dust. Long before this Li Po was virtually
dismissed the Court, for characteristic mis-
demeanours, by which much loss of " face " was
caused in official quarters. He had even ordered
the Eunuch-in-Chief to pull off his boots for
him when he was drunk.

There are poems of his where some rumbles of
the storm that had destroyed Hsuan Tsung can
be heard, a far and melancholy sound, after the
end had come :

" *Flute notes complaining* . . .
In the pavilions of Ch'in young girls sleepless under the moon,
Under the moon.
Year upon year willows at Paling lament separation.

On Loyu terrace it's mid-Autumn,
And the old road to Hsien Yang[1] *is hidden beneath dark dust,*
Dark dust.
There's a west wind and dim light over the royal tombs of Han."

We roused ourselves presently, stretched our
stiff backs, and called for more tea. Then we
hired a boat and rowed placidly round the edge
of the cliff. It was a radiant evening; the
Yangtze waters lapped and flowed a thick purple
and copper. About the time when the cottage
chimneys in the village below began to puff out
their individual smoke, in promise of the evening
meal, we strolled back to the station. On the
other side of the line peasants were still planting
out the young rice. Some threw bundles of the
seedlings at regular intervals into the watery
mud, and others separated and planted with
rapid, decisive movements—fascinating to watch,
so sure, effective, rhythmic was every action :
traditional toil. The whole field, a small one, was
planted while we waited for the train. It was
dark when we reached Nanking.

All this happened in the spring of 1936, and
I thought many times afterwards of Li Po's
cynically humorous figure in its bright trappings,

[1] Sometimes identified with Ch'ang An.

thought of the well-chosen scenery, the poems, and the *bonhomie*, the sublime and the ridiculous astonishingly compounded. I compared with them so many of our poets' shrines in the West, glass-cased and documented, and I wonder whether in our unpardonable pompousness we have not overlooked many a good chance.

A few days ago I pulled open a drawer, and there on top lay a Chinese silk fan, a kingfisher painted on it. There was even a whiff of incense among its scarlet paper wrappings. Remembered sensations of sight and sound sprang up with the perfume—the temple on the rock, the waters, the incense-sticks toppling their dead ash in segments on to the altar. It was a strangely moving moment, for at that very time newsboys at London street-corners were yelling " Japanese troops at the walls of Nanking ! "

That night I was late in sleeping. I dreamt I saw the statue of my Chinese friend—a cherished companion of Oxford days, with whom I afterwards lived in China—set in a red pagoda on the edge of a cliff. A wind was roaring with terrifying noise and force, and I felt if it blew me from the sight of her face we should be separated for ever. I struggled in desperation to keep my footing, but while I watched, the statue began to crumble ; its hangings of bright beads trickled off on to the ground, and the whole image began slowly to lose shape of human form. Mercifully that was the point for waking. I turned on the light violently and tried to rid myself of the horrible memory by pulling out a volume of Li Po, the poet who never died, but as some say, rejoined the Immortals riding on the back of a whale. Among the poems I found the following ; its heart-sickness can hardly be caught in translation :

> " *Last year's battle*
>   *At San Kan spring.*
>   *This year*
>   *Tsung Ho road.*
> *We've washed our armour in lake waves of Chiao-Chih,*
> *Pastured our horses on Heaven's Mountain, the snow-flecked grass ;*
> *We've fought across ten thousand miles,*
> *Three armies exhausted and become old men.*
>
> *The barbarian's plough cuts through bodies of the slaughtered,*
> *For years bones whitened yellow sandy fields ;*
> *Where Chin Emperors piled walls against the Tartars*
> *Han men are burning beacon fires.*
> *Their flames lick and burn without sinking—*
>   *War never ends.*
>
> *In the battle-wastes men grapple and die,*
> *Horses of the fallen neigh pitifully to heaven,*
> *Kites and ravens peck at human entrails—*
> *Lift them in their beaks and hang them from withered branches,*
> *Soldiers' bodies are smeared on the desert grass. . . .*
>   *The generals are unvictorious—*
>   *What's the use of their engines of war ?*
>   *The Sages of old found no purpose for them.*"

CHINA AND DEMOCRACY

H. J. Laski

JAPANESE aggression in China is one of a series of attacks upon the foundations of post-war civilisation which threatens to inaugurate a new dark age. The principles upon which it is conducted are not merely a breach of international treaties; they are also incompatible with any attempt at international organisation. They assume the right of any nation-state to make war a deliberate instrument of national policy. They assume, further, that the relations between states are simply a question of power, and their inner logic is built upon the premiss that what power may effect is entitled to acceptance as right. A Japanese victory would not merely be the admission that the relations between states are incapable of being organised— the virtual coronation of anarchy in international relations. It would also be the acceptance of the view that the moralisation of state-policy is not a legitimate object for statesmen to pursue since it would be void of any basis in practical life.

It is the implications of all this that we have to

consider in our attitude to Japan. Its victory over China would mean that no nation against whom another nation had a grievance of any kind would feel safe from aggression. It would, therefore, compel every nation in this position to rely for its future solely upon the material strength of which it could dispose. Clearly enough, this means a great armaments race, of which, as we know, the outcome is insecurity, reciprocal suspicion, and, in the long run, war. But because it means these things, it involves also the devotion of a large proportion of the national expenditure to defence ; and this, in its turn, means, as Mr. Chamberlain has frequently emphasised, the postponement of any profound schemes of social reform. This is bound to have the effect of imposing a severe strain on the domestic life of the modern nation-state, since the effectiveness of its government is largely dependent upon its ability to raise the standard of life of its people. Japanese policy, to put it shortly, proceeds by methods which guarantee the advent of an epoch of international war and social revolution. They limit the prospect of confronting the essential problems of the modern state in a rational way. For by relying upon force as the arbiter of destiny, they deprive reason and justice of their empire over the minds of men.

The implications of the dispute cannot be confined to the aggressor and its victim. They strike a blow at important commercial interests of other nations which, sooner or later, are bound to be defended. Thereby their effect is cumulative. For the result of the threat to commercial interests is necessarily the need to take steps in their defence. This sets up a chain of causation with ramifications all over the world. And its consequences are not limited to the sphere Japan seeks to dominate. Every nation-state which has claims, real or imaginary, which it seeks to satisfy, watches the progress of the Japanese adventure. It builds its policy upon the inferences it draws from that progress. Exactly as the conquest of Manchuria in 1931-2 stimulated Hitler and Mussolini, so their breaches of international law have, in their turn, stimulated Fascist intervention in Spain ; and the success of this effort has led the Japanese to believe that they can go farther on the road to the conquest of China with impunity.

The deterioration in the international position which results from this identification of power with right is almost incalculable. It compels each nation-state which believes itself to be threatened—and all believe themselves to be threatened—to take precautions lest it be the next victim of aggressive attack. Those precautions mean rearmament on an ever-increasing scale ; and the need to prepare against war not only slows down all processes of social beneficence but also jeopardises the maintenance of the democratic fabric by the inroads war compels on the normal habits of a population. For there is entailed in the preparations even for war a system of priorities which compel relentlessly the subordination of rational habits to ends which are themselves the denial of reason. The building of houses is sacrificed to the building of aeroplanes; the extension of services for maternity and child welfare is cancelled lest it interfere with the extension of precautions against the effect of air raids. The need for more education gives way to the need for more guns.

Anyone, in short, who studies in detail the consequences of Japanese aggression in China cannot but perceive that it is one of those major events which may well be a turning-point for evil in the history of civilisation. It is not merely that the aggression attempted is so wholly disproportionate to the provocation received. It is not even the cynical violation by the Japanese of solemn commitments, the full observance of which was the cement of international good faith. It is, still more than these, the vital fact that the success of this provocation is an incentive and an encouragement to all the dark forces of our civilisation who will use the precedent, if it be allowed to establish itself, as the basis upon which to attempt similar adventures of their own. Forces are being unleashed in the world the loosing of which will destroy all the standards of behaviour which make life worth living.

There are few people in Great Britain prepared to condone what Japan has done. But there are too few who see, as they ought to see, in the fate of China, a threat also to ourselves. If a powerful nation is allowed to run amok, merely because it is powerful, there is no other nation that can regard itself as safe ; to recognise as legitimate the claim of the gangster, pursued by the methods of the gangster, is to invite a universal threat to security. Because this is the case, the cause of China is our own cause. In vindicating her right to be free from aggressive attack, we are assisting to establish the principle that aggression in itself cannot be condoned. More than this, by a refusal to assist China we become guilty of connivance in the victory of Japan. We proclaim our indifference to the use of methods the inherent barbarity of which we are ourselves solemnly pledged to condemn. Upon ourselves that has two results which are wholly evil. It leads us to persuade ourselves that the methods are less evil than we know them to be ; and it accustoms us to indifference in the presence of evil as we encounter it. We degrade ourselves by the condonation of methods we know to be indefensible.

Our generation, no doubt, has been habituated to horror by the constancy of its occurrence. What we do not seem sufficiently to have understood is that the constancy is in large part the outcome of our acquiescence to that habituation. We have so often, in the post-war years, sought to find reasons for indifference, that we are in danger of becoming indifferent without regard to the price that we pay for our behaviour. It is not, I think, political bias, but an objective judgment of the facts to say that the decline of our international influence in recent years is very largely the outcome of the belief in aggressive states that we are not to be accounted an active agent in the arrest of their wrong. We have, no doubt, proclaimed our faith in collective security and the Covenant of the League of Nations. But it has been assumed abroad—not without reason—that the proclamation was contingent upon the understanding that we had not to implement our faith. The great tests of Manchuria, of the Rhineland, and of Abyssinia, found us either cynical or half-hearted. We gave the impression that our word was not our bond. Aggressive powers have acted upon that impression. We have seen, in consequence, the abandonment of the rule of law and its replacement by the rule of force. We know that, in the end, the rule of force means an international disaster in which we ourselves will be involved. The inference is surely the clear one that we must take all steps we can take to prevent the coming of disaster.

We are confronted by a Japanese imperialism which threatens to set the whole world in flames. We cannot arrest the conflagration by notes of protest which, though duly followed by apology, never stem the flow of incidents which cause them. It is obvious to the most casual observer that the purpose of these incidents is the calculated one of compelling the Chinese to realise that the Western Powers are helpless and thereby to break, if possible, the spirit of resistance. Those who depend upon the politics of power are not moved by protests which remain in the realm of the spirit. What they understand is the deed and not the word. A Japan which has reduced China to the status of a vassal will be prepared for endless protests ; for none of them will interfere with the end it has in view.

The true lesson of the Japanese adventure is that the only path of safety for this country lies in the path of collective security. Admittedly, we cannot, in the circumstances of the international situation, seek to fight Japan alone. But, at least, we can, in concert with other powers, lead the way to action which would imperil the Japanese position. We control her economic future. Her dependence upon other powers for raw materials, not least the raw materials of war, her need to export manufactured goods and silk, if she is to maintain her financial position, these show that there is no necessity for impotent acquiescence in her aggression. The power of the international boycott is one which the very dangers of the present position makes it imperative to use. The alternative to its use now is to serve notice upon the aggressor that his might is equivalent to his right. That is tantamount to an invitation to every dissatisfied nation in the world to seek by might to assuage its dissatisfaction. The evidence accumulates that they will profit by the invitation; and there is no one who is unaware that the outcome is bound to be world-war.

It is said that to adopt the policy of economic boycott will merely drive Japan to further aggression. It is possible. But it is a risk that we are bound to take unless we assume the validity of non-resistance in every circumstance. That is not the premiss of our Government's policy. Because it is not, the major consideration we have to bear in mind is that the risk involved in trying to stop Japan now is far smaller than the risk of seeking to arrest a Japan which has assumed control of Chinese resources and, so far, rendered herself independent of the raw materials of Europe and America. It is, indeed, unlikely that the attempt will be made, once China has been reduced to the status of a Japanese colony. Rather will her victory be used as an excuse for those within our own country to whom any success is an excuse for wrong, and

F

to those without who are eager for a Japanese victory as the proof that they may safely emulate her example elsewhere. If we are to act, the time for action is now, when there is at least the hope that courage may be followed by results.

We ought to remember, moreover, that we are witnessing a deliberate effort on the part of a militarist autocracy to stifle a nascent Chinese democracy before it has the chance to attain a full self-consciousness. To assist that new democracy to affirm itself is on every ground in our own interest—if our Government means what it says by its protestations in favour of democracy. An independent China is the greatest safeguard we can have of peace in the Far East. It is, also, the greatest assurance available that the normal opportunities of commercial intercourse will continue to be available to other nations than Japan. The growth of democracy in China will be, as the parallel evolution of the Soviet Union has shown, in itself an encouragement to peace. Little else, moreover, can be regarded as so grave a setback to the pretensions of Fascist imperialism elsewhere. Those pretensions grow by what they feed on. That has been shown, not only in the case of Japan itself, but, also, of Mussolini and Hitler. To attain their ambitions, they are prepared to risk setting the world in flames. They constitute, at the

present time, a menace to peace which can only
be removed by objective and demonstrable
proof that a policy of aggression does not pay.
So far, we have refused to take the risks of offering
that proof, with the result that, all over the
world, we have contributed enormously to
the enhancement of the prestige of Fascist
imperialism.

It is no answer to this argument to say that a
policy of collective security has broken down,
that the League is in ruins, and that it is useless
to count upon American support. The policy
of collective security has never been tried in
conditions which offered it the least prospect of
success. In every major crisis since 1919, the
use of the League has been deliberately evaded;
and it must be added with regret that none has
contributed more to that evasion than the
Government of Great Britain. American support
for a policy of economic boycott cannot be
deemed impossible until it has been sought.
It must be remembered that in 1931 the Government of the United States was willing to concert
measures with Great Britain to call a halt to the
Japanese occupation of Manchuria. It was
Great Britain then which repulsed the offer. The
Chicago speech of President Roosevelt is evidence
and to spare of his awareness of the great issues
that are in dispute. It is illegitimate to conclude
that its principles were empty phrase-making

until we have definitely sought to build concrete action upon them.

There are some who say that a bold policy on our part must wait until our programme of rearmament is completed. But on that view there are at least two things to be said. In a real way a rearmament programme is never complete, since it is never a unilateral adventure. It depends for its level of attainment upon forces outside our control. If we wait until then, we shall have no alternative but to accept whatever Japan seeks to impose upon China as her terms. And, in any case, if we wait, it is at least probable that when we feel ready to act, the Japanese conquest of China will be a *fait accompli*. The task of arrest will then obviously be more difficult: it is, indeed, doubtful if, in those circumstances, it would be attempted.

It is said that a policy of economic boycott, such as is here recommended, is one that involves us in the risk of war. Englishmen, it is said, cannot attempt to police the world; they have enough to do with their own concerns. That there is the risk of war in this policy is undeniable. But it is also true that there is, even if in the long run, the greater risk of an even more disastrous war without it. To abandon China, as we are in fact abandoning it, is to give decisive encouragement to exactly those forces in the world to whose development the British people are one of the few remaining obstacles. To abandon China now is to assist in its surrender to a power that has deliberately chosen to become the ally of the anti-democratic powers of Western Europe. It is to offer them the prospect of using that alliance for an aggression that is bound to involve ourselves. It is true that we take a risk ; but, as things are, we take it upon ground where there is hope of a far lesser danger than when the next action occurs.

Englishmen cannot police the world. That also is true ; and no one can expect Great Britain to give aid alone to the Chinese people. What can be expected, and what is here demanded, is that Great Britain take the initiative in pressing upon the powers to whom peace is still a major interest the necessity of acting together against an aggressor who has elevated hypocrisy and cruelty into deliberate principles of policy. There is evidence and to spare that when, as at Nyon, Great Britain takes the initiative in an enterprise of this kind, not only are other states willing to give her their support, but those states against whom the initiative is taken do not venture the risks involved in its defiance. More than this. It was shown at the time of the Hoare-Laval proposals that there is a great volume of opinion in this country which takes seriously its responsibilities to the League of Nations and is prepared to support a government which is

willing also to take them seriously. To confine
British policy to no more than the defence of
direct imperial interests will not unite the nation,
but divide it. What alone, to many of us, seems
worth while in the light of the Great War, is to
take action in defence of those principles which
offer the maximum assurance against its recur-
rence. The central feature of those principles is
the idea of collective security. Japanese aggression threatens that idea as it has not been
threatened since the war. To prove that the
authority of Great Britain is behind it is the one
sure way of giving it the chance of translation
from concept to fact.

I have said nothing here of the massive brutality
with which the Japanese onslaught upon China
has been conducted. I have said nothing, either,
of the calculated effort to destroy all that China
has sought to build, not least her educational
institutions, in that remarkable effort at self-
regeneration which has been the central feature
of her recent history. That brutality and that
destruction are an inherent part of Fascist imperialism wherever it is found. They mark its
inability to reconcile itself with all normal
standards of humanity and culture of which it is
the permanent foe. Fascist imperialism is, by its
own immanent logic, brutal and barbaric. It is
compelled by its inherent compulsion to transform all it can dominate into its own image. The

more extensive its authority, the more fragile become the defences of what is best in our traditional civilisation. It cannot be too emphatically insisted that nothing less than those defences are in jeopardy. History has made China to-day a central bulwark in those defences. To assist her in this grave hour is to strengthen them at a pivotal point. To risk her subjection to an arrogant imperialism is to weaken them just at the point where they cause profound repercussions upon ourselves. The situation is one where our duty and interest alike concur to enforce the same lesson. To make a stand now against the advancing tide of barbarism may be our salvation. To-morrow it may be too late.

I have sought in these pages to refrain deliberately from the use of any word to which people who do not share my own political faith could take exception. I believe that the character of Japanese aggression in China is repulsive to all British subjects, indifferently to the party to which they may belong. I believe, further, that the urgency of preventing its victory transcends, in the consequences it makes possible, all differences which divide the nation. In this conflict, it cannot be argued too strongly, the fate of the whole world is involved. The victim is China to-day ; if she is left to perish, it is as certain as the rising of the sun that there will be another victim to-morrow. We have the opportunity, as we have the obligation, to take action for international principles which post-war history has shown are the essential condition of peace. We may, if we so will, not only save ourselves by our energy ; we may also, if we so choose, save civilisation by our example. I pray that we may have a courage proportionate to our responsibilities in this grave hour.

THE CHURCH FACES THE STORM

Basil Mathews

AS I try to visualise the Chinese Christian communities trying to keep their feet in the tornado now sweeping over their country, the memory rises before me of a slim, blue-gowned Chinese scholar talking with a group of us in Oxford in the summer of 1937, just when that storm was breaking. He said : " I have seen my boyhood friends wiped out in Shanghai. . . . I have in my home in Peiping for five months watched five columns of Japanese armies moving on us. I have seen four provinces taken from my country. What do I, as a Christian, say to that ? "

" First," he continued, " as a person redeemed by Christ I am conscious of power to incarnate the will of God into human relations. Political organisations have repeatedly failed us. Chinese youth thrilled to Wilson's Fourteen Points. The Versailles Treaty dashed this to the ground. When Japan took Manchuria our hopes were in the League of Nations. Again it all went flop. In the Abyssinian crisis we saw Eden, a knight in flashing armour, and again—flop. We Christians dare not put before the world a tremendous gas-bag to be pricked.

" Let us," he said, " work on what we have to say and do ourselves. As an individual I don't say whether I will fight or not, but I am steadily working at how to love my enemy—and the Japanese are sitting," he said with grim humour, " on my family doorstep waiting to be loved. They bring opium to that doorstep and insist on me and my family buying it on pain of my being denounced as a Communist.

" Then I must interweave into all my living the greater loyalty that gathers up the lesser loyalties. My ultimate loyalty is to the Kingdom of God. So, personally, I am trying to be a Christian in spite of my experience.

" As a Christian member of the world community," he pursued his argument, " because it is a world of sin, I must work for a new world. I must create an international outlook when my nation is emphasising nationalistic education for the young. I must stand for co-operation when my nation may stand for absolute sovereignty. That sovereignty must be subordinated to social ends."

The Christian communities in China for whom these problems are so urgent and personal are largely the growth of the past century. Robert Morrison, the first Protestant missionary to China, landed in 1807. Their membership is sparsely scattered among the villages in all the provinces of China and in numbers of its cities. The Roman Catholic Church claims nearly two and three-quarter million members and has stated that in 1936 about half a million new members were baptised. The Protestant and Anglican Christian communities now include about a million adherents. The National Christian Council of China represents 61 per cent of the latter churches, and is responsible during recent years for a striking development of closer co-operation and a settled will for unity. Its general secretary, Dr. W. Y. Chen, educated in China, America, England, France, and Germany, is at the head of a staff of ten secretaries, of whom five are Chinese. The work of the Council covers, as one of its secretaries, Mr. Ronald Rees, says in his book just off the press, *China Faces the Storm*,[1] the whole field of Church life including education and medicine.

Our concern here is not with the historic past of the Christian Church in China, but with its contemporary life in the setting of the world Christian community, as it faces the present crisis.

The Christian movement in China rounded a difficult curve during the decade from 1928 to 1938. As a result the Christian forces are now much more closely aligned toward a unified

[1] Edinburgh House Press, 1937.

policy and programme, and that programme bears more directly upon the future of the Chinese people. This change, which does not lack dramatic episodes, may best be visualised by focusing the situation that confronted the able group of Chinese Christian leaders as they sailed together from Jerusalem to China in 1928. They had been deliberating upon the world strategy of Christianity with their peers from all over the world at the enlarged meeting of the International Missionary Council on the Mount of Olives.

That group included five personalities whose outstanding qualities of character, intellect, and vision gave them an ascendancy even in such a world gathering of picked leaders from every continent as that in which they had just shared. Dr. Cheng Ching-yi was Moderator of the Church of Christ in China, a Church that is now in process of fusing into one community some sixteen denominations whose affiliations run back into British, European, and American sectarianism. President Francis Wei of the Central China Christian University, in addition to the leadership which he gives in education, is bending his ripe scholarship to explore the congruity of the Confucian ethical system with that of Jesus Christ. Professor T. C. Chao, through his integration of the cultural and artistic life of China as well as the metaphysical hinterland of her ethics to the Christian religion, is laying foundations for an indigenous Christian movement. The late Dr. David Yui[1] was one of the truly great men among the leaders of the world's Christian youth movements. Miss Pao-sen Tseng, a descendant of the disciple who, two and a half thousand years ago, kept the lamp of Confucius' teaching alight and is a great-granddaughter of Tseng Kuo-fan, the great patriot statesman, is herself the creator of the Garden of Fragrance school at Changsha, in Central China, which is developing a new leadership of Christian young womanhood from families that are the flower of Chinese culture.

The perils and sufferings that China, and particularly the Christian Church, were facing in 1928 challenged this group of leaders to make some courageous and far-sighted attack upon the problem. In great areas remote from this clash Chinese peasant life pursued its usual course. Nationalist and Communist armies were marching and counter-marching across the land. Miss Tseng's school, however, lay in the path of conflict. It had been smashed first by the Nationalist and then by the Communist armies, and she was on her return to take up the work of rebuilding. Massacre, looting, the laying waste of crops, and

[1] David Yui collapsed in 1931 at the end of a long interview with Mr. Stimson, then Secretary of State at Washington, and never recovered. The strain of the Japanese invasion has thus robbed China of one of its great builders of new citizenship.

the burning down of homes spelt starvation for those who eluded the rifle or the bayonet. These miseries were crowned by the horror of flood bursting through neglected dykes. The China of those years was a scene of desolation across which galloped the Four Horsemen of the Apocalypse—war, famine, pestilence, and death.

These terrors smote all alike—Christian and non-Christian : but upon the Christian Church came an added misery. Nationalists were anti-Christian in 1928 because they believed that Christianity was the handmaid of foreign imperialism. Communism was on principle anti-Christian. Processions of youth on both sides carried such banners as : " Down with Christianity, the opiate of the oppressed," or : " Down with Christianity, the means of cultural aggression." Girls and women in these processions carried banners with such slogans as : " Down with male domination," and : " Down with Christianity, the oppressor of womanhood." Christian churches in areas overrun by the Communist armies were burned to the ground or, if left standing, the name was painted out and the old cliché of " Religion the opiate " painted up on the wall. Pastors were taken by Nationalist groups and paraded round city or village with a notice hung round their necks such as : " I am the running-dog of the foreigner." A number of pastors were hanged.

Christian village churches were broken up;
but they were not destroyed. They were purged,
of course, of the half-hearted, and many local
leaders were lost through death and dispersal;
but the remnant, meeting like the Church of the
first century in the houses of the faithful, threw
deeper roots into the soil.

Dr. Cheng Ching-yi, as chairman of the
National Christian Council of China, reinforced
by Dr. John R. Mott, called the Christian leaders
together in province after province and then in
a National Council meeting. The aim was, in
his own phrase, to get the Church " out of
the trenches " into the open field for advance.
Taking as background a Chinese word for
" crisis " that combines the two characters
" danger " and " opportunity," and with the
prayer " Lord, revive thy Church, beginning
with me " as central to all their work, the " Jesus
Church "[1] launched a Five-Year Movement on a
five-fold front. The five objectives were : first,
evangelism, by personal work, preaching, literature, films, and broadcasting ; secondly, literacy
in the Church, in which Dr. Yen's thousand-
character system, to be described later, was of
high value ; thirdly, religion in the home—which
in China above all places is the inexpugnable
centre of reality ; fourthly, education in the

[1] The Roman Catholic Church is known as " the Lord
of Heaven Church."

practice of the presence of God, to serve which a
" religious education fellowship " was formed ;
and fifthly, the christianisation of the economic
and social life of rural and industrial China.
From America and Europe came help through
men and women of prophetic and interpretative
gifts.

While the Christian community in this way
laid hold of its task, the antagonism to Christianity from Nationalist and Communist groups
diminished. This improvement in the atmosphere was due in part to the fact that the leadership of Chinese Christianity passed with increasing
speed into capable patriotic Chinese hands, thus
robbing the charge of imperialism of even
surface plausibility.

Simultaneously, certain Chinese Christians and
men with strong Christian affiliations moved to a
prominence and a national influence in political
and economic reconstruction out of all proportion to the size or the prestige of the Christian
Church in the nation. Of Chinese political
leaders to-day a very large number were educated
in the West. They run into two distinct groups.
Those educated in Europe are, for the most part,
completely secular in their thought and either
purely critical of Christianity or definitely hostile
to it. Those educated in America and Britain
are, to a considerable extent, sympathetic to
Christianity and, in a good number of cases, are

convinced practising members of Protestant Churches.

We might cite many examples. A few will suffice. Dr. Cheng-ting Wang, the ambassador to Washington, is the son of a Christian minister. He taught in the Anglo-Chinese College at Tientsin under the London Missionary Society and became Christian Student Movement secretary to Chinese students in Tokyo. After some years in American Universities he became national secretary to the Y.M.C.A. in China. He then threw in his lot with Dr. Sun Yat-sen, became one of the principal delegates of China at the Versailles Conference in 1919, became Foreign Minister in the Nationalist Government and was successful in negotiating treaties that freed China from many humiliating territorial concessions. By his reasonable, though persistent, temper he compelled the respect even of those who opposed his aims. Mr. Wang Chung-hui, Chinese Minister for Foreign Affairs, is the son of a Christian minister and is a distinguished lawyer, having represented China at The Hague Court. Dr. W. W. Yen, who has successively been Foreign Minister and Prime Minister and then ambassador to Soviet Russia, and his brother, and Mr. F. T. Yen, Vice-Minister of Railways, are Christians, as are such leading members of the Legislative Council (the equivalent to our Parliament) as its president, Mr. Sun Fo, son of Dr. Sun Yat-sen,

Dr. C. L. Hsia, the jurist and treasurer of the
National Christian Council, and that brilliant
intellect and courageous will in the weakest of
bodies, Dr. Timothy Tingfang Lew. A survey
of the provincial governments would give
similar examples.

Most conspicuous of all among Chinese members of the Christian Church is, of course, the
Soong family, with its two famous brothers and
three forceful sisters married to famous men.
Madam Chiang is most in the eye of the world
these days as she stands by her husband's side at
the centre of the raging storm. But that sacri-
ficial figure, Madam Sun, widow to the " Dead
Leader," has her own place deep in the hearts of
her own people. And then there is Madam Kung
and her husband, Dr. H. H. Kung, both strong
supporters of the Christian Church. Dr. Kung
and his brother-in-law, Mr. T. V. Soong, have
both held the post of Finance Minister to the
Nanking Government. " T.V." is the guiding
and inspiring chairman of the National Economic
Council whose contribution to China's life is
described by Sir Arthur Salter in another chapter
of this book. Dr. Kung, in Europe, successfully
negotiated railway loans with France and other
governments. Early in 1938 he became Premier
of the National Government of China. When
Chiang Kai-shek and his wife started the New
Life Movement for lifting the habits and social

life of the rank and file of China to a higher level,
they not only appealed to the National Christian
Council for co-operation, but chose a Chinese
Christian as the first general secretary and have
placed alongside him a missionary from New
Zealand. So also in the National Child Welfare
Association, and other forward-looking movements, Christians have supplied the initiating
force.

It would, of course, in China, as in any country,
be easy to point to nominal Christians whose
character has not stood the strain of political or
economic temptation ; and to criticise the work
of those mentioned here. The significance of
these personalities lies in the double fact that the
nation knows that they have been through the
Christian mill and that they represent the force
which Christianity is, in its strength as in its
weakness. They contribute an intellectual power
and ability to deal with men and situations. They
are not haloed saints, but they are exploring their
ways, as we can see from the account of the
Generalissimo's vigil in Hsian last Christmas.
They have the capacity to learn from the blows
which beat on their heads. Is it too much to say
that through their faith they are the more able to
make the cruel decisions which must be made
to-day ?

To-day the Christian communities in China
have fifty thousand boys and girls in secondary

schools and seven thousand students in colleges.
Those communities and the missionary forces
that serve them have to-day a more coherent and
intense consciousness of responsibility for training the citizens the country needs, among them
men and women capable of far-sighted, principled
handling of the executive and diplomatic tasks
that will be decisive for her future.

Three further illuminating examples may be
given of this creative contribution to the making
of a new China. They illustrate the function of
the Christian community as " leaven."

Dr. James Yen, a young Christian graduate
from West China, who was in training for a
diplomatic career, went with the Chinese coolies
to France in the Great War. Their agonised
home-sickness and boredom led him to try and
teach them to write. He began the sifting process
by which, on returning to China, he reduced the
thirty thousand " characters " of the literary
language to a basic thousand. His eye was upon
the 80 per cent of Chinese peasantry who are
wholly or partly illiterate. He created the
National Association for the Advancement of
Mass Education. To-day not only more than a
million adult persons have learned to read, but
alongside the new literacy of these small farmers
goes health, education, preventive medicine, the
breeding of better fowl and pigs, the use of tested
seeds, and pioneer work in the introduction of

goats to add milk to the diet of rural China. This system has been pushed forward on the one side by the National Government and on the other by the National Christian Council in its Five-Year Movement already described. It is used in the fortnightly paper, *The Christian Farmer,* which reaches some 350,000 readers and is ably edited by Mr. T. H. Sun of the National Christian Council.

This leads us to the second example of leaven in the mass of the life of China. One of the notable young graduates of St. John's University, Shanghai, and Yale University, is Mr. Chang Fu-liang, who threw his unusual abilities, from 1929 onward, into the rural reconstruction movement of the National Christian Council. With the approval of the Government and the consent of the local authorities groups of villages are taken. The Christian Church serves each group as a single community. Pastors, who are being trained to teach the farmers what the Gospel is, bring home to them the truth of the preaching by helping them to fight the malaria and hook-worm that are the cause of so much listlessness and fatalism, to secure disease-free silkworm eggs, and roosters whose progeny will produce two hundred and fifty eggs a year in contrast with sixty from the average lethargic hen. Meanwhile the pastor's wife helps the peasant women to transform their homes by a more scientific knowledge of the nourishment of children and elementary domestic hygiene. And with the help of Dr. Yen's system they meanwhile are moving for the first time on the continent of Asia toward a literate Church. And mark this: Toyohiko Kagawa, the great Japanese Christian social reformer, is gratefully acknowledged by many Christian social workers in China as the man who has inspired them. His particular rural co-operative programme is regarded by many liberal Chinese—as also liberal Japanese—as the true alternative to ideological Communism.

The third creative contribution of the Christian Church in China in this decade of crisis lies in the persistence of its leaders in trying to sustain the bridge of genuine international comradeship, that bridge which Japanese Christian leaders have helped to build, not without danger to themselves. Even in the spring of 1937 a Sino-Japanese group entered into a retreat for fellowship together, while those who were present at Oxford in June, 1937, at the World Conference on Church, Community, and State will recall the presence of Japanese and Chinese together in the discussions and at the celebration of Holy Communion. "I am a loyal Chinese," said a Christian, "and I hate the policy which Japan is carrying out in China with all my soul, but I shall go on working for Christian brotherhood between our peoples."

The National Government, during the ten years leading up to 1938, brought into effective being the organism, however rudimentary, of a modern State, using the technical skill of international well-wishers, as Sir Arthur Salter has shown elsewhere in this volume. Similarly, as we have now seen, the Christian Church, working through the National Christian Council, shaped and carried forward, in that same decade, a national policy and programme calculated to feed the soul, guide the conscience, and strengthen the hands of the new China.

The titanic blows that Japan has in 1937 inflicted upon the body and soul of China affect in a peculiar degree the fortunes of that growing Christian community. Obviously the impact of any ruthless invasion in itself inflicts a severe shock upon the Church. In this case, however, a circumstance, surely unique in modern history, lifts the argument to a level like that of Greek drama. Nerving the arm of Japan, we see the towering dæmonic spirit of the Divine State. The modern cult of Shinto has in Japan lifted the will of the State above all rivals. " Cæsar is God." Nowhere, even in the totalitarian States of Europe, has the worship of the State been carried to such mystical and logical perfection as in Japan. From the first century in Ephesus and Rome up till the twentieth century in Berlin and Tokyo, Christians have never been able to

surrender the loyalty involved in the words,
" I believe in God the Father Almighty." These
two " absolutes " now face each other in the
Far East. Such an imperial rule as that of ancient
Rome or of modern Japan seems always to be
blinded to the fact that Christ's command
" Render unto Cæsar the things that are Cæsar's,
and unto God the things that are God's " made
and makes Christians the best of all citizens.
For in so far as they are loyal to that creative
Spirit who is above the State, they bring to the
service of their nation just those qualities that
preserve it from corruption.

When we ask then through what fortunes the
Christian community in China will be likely to
pass in the near future, it would be foolish to
dogmatise. In the light, however, of the severity
including imprisonment and even torture meted
out in Manchuria to Chinese Christians innocent
of all rebellious speech or action, we can hardly
expect that Chinese in the areas controlled by
Japanese military occupation will escape the
subtle forms of modern martyrdom imposed by
the totalitarian State. The words of teachers,
the writing of textbooks, and other processes
are used forcibly to mould men within a steel
cage that imprisons them and often ultimately
atrophies even the wings of freedom.

In the areas of China that remain outside
Japanese control no forecast can be expressed

with any confidence. There are, however,
certain considerations that we do well to hold in
mind.

If under the stress of nationalistic ardour
the wine of Fascism should mount to the head
of a vehement and able Chinese group, and if
as a result the Government became Fascist we
should expect to see the familiar attitude of the
totalitarian State to the Christian Church.

If, on the other hand, the so-called Communist
forces, as a reward for the help that they now
render to the national cause and because of their
unquestioned military capacity, rose to the top,
our view would be that the Christian Church
will probably have little to fear. What is called
Communist rule in China mainly consists in
tearing up the title-deeds of the landlord and
confirming the peasant in his tenure of the land
that he tills, subject to his payment of taxes and
to loyal behaviour. Of the teachings of Karl Marx
or the apothegms of Lenin neither the peasants
nor their " Red " rulers have any profound knowledge. The alliance of the " Communist " forces
with the liberal social democracy of the Kuomintang to resist Japan has softened the edge of
earlier asperity. Japan would be nearer than
ever to their frontiers. For these reasons we may
anticipate tolerance of the differing faiths of all
good citizens. Indeed, we might see the Christian
Church in China freed from that net of middle-

class commercial mentality which is in China, as in the Western world, the chief danger for the Church.

If, however, Chiang Kai-shek and those who work with him are able to hold together the amalgam of different forces on a moderate central platform, neither Fascist nor Communist, and carry forward a democratic programme, the Church might well, through the Christian leadership that we have briefly described, make in the future a still greater contribution to the guidance of the nation and the State; and through its rank and file be a spiritual and moral leaven in the great and free China that, sooner or later, must have that great place among the nations which is her due.

THE LITTLE GOD

Eileen Power

A true tale telling how a little god that lived in a temple on the road leading from Peking to the Western Hills, having failed to provide rain, was put out under the scorching rays of the sun, and how rain thereafter mysteriously fell in torrents.

THE little god lived in a temple on the road which leads from Peking into the Western Hills. The temple had walls painted a dim rose colour, and its roof was made of shining yellow tiles. The little god sat in a room in a small courtyard, with green and blue and golden beams above his head, and every day people came in and lighted sticks of sweet-smelling incense before him, which they stuck upright in the soft grey ash left by all the sticks which had burned down before. It was only a poor and unpretentious temple, and the little god was not a very important little god. He sat cross-legged and smiled an inscrutable smile, with one hand raised, and the dull golden lacquer with which he was covered had gone a little thin in places. Still, he was a god, and the people who lived in his village were wont to explain to him their simple, but insistent, needs, and in particular the great need they had every year, in the summer season, of rain to make their crops of corn and millet and sorghum grow.

When the harvest was safely gathered in, the people would come and burn an extra stick or two of incense and bring the little god three or four cracked china bowls full of cooked millet and bean curd, or other food which they thought he would like. It was nothing compared with the fine array of candles and dishes which stood before the great Buddha in the Lama Temple in Peking; nor could it compare with the rows of tiny shoes and clay babies which women brought to the goddess Kwan Yin, who sat with her child on her knee in the Temple-with-the-Upside-Down-Shadow just outside the City gate; but then, he was only a little god. The great Buddha heard all the sorrows and desires of men, the prayers of politicians who wished to make a private fortune out of their offices of State, the complaints of Manchu dukes, who had lost their lands in the revolution; the ambitions of slim-handed actors, who wanted to win the favour of the young men of Peking by acting languorous women on the stage; therefore it was meet that the incense-sticks before the great Buddha should be two feet high and the number of his food-bowls thirty. And the goddess Kwan Yin heard

all the sorrows and desires of women; the pain
of little girls, when the cruel bandages pressed
their tender feet, in order that one day they might
win husbands; the whispers of dark-eyed ladies,
with flowers in their hair and powder on their
cheeks, who wanted lovers; the tears of deserted
wives cast away like an old fan; and the aching
need of mothers without children; therefore the
images and the tiny shoes clustered round the
throne where Kwan Yin sat. But the little god
had none of these things to do. He had only
to send the rain, and his simple task brought only
simple offerings.

As a rule, the little god performed his duties
very satisfactorily, and the sun shone and the
rain fell in due season, so that the crops ripened.
But one blazing summer the villagers looked
day after day anxiously at the sky and saw no
cloud and no sign of rain. The earth was baked
hard, and although they turned what water
they could upon it down their tiny irrigation
channels, it became dry again at once and great
cracks appeared upon its surface. The crops
languished and drooped for want of drink and
could not burst into ear. Under the sparse shade
of the gingko trees the village dogs lay panting,
with their tongues hanging from their jaws, and
the patient donkeys drooped their necks and
seemed hardly able to support themselves upon
their slender legs. Day after day the villagers

saw famine come nearer to them, the terrible
famine of North China, when men's bones stick
out of their skins and little children can hardly
crawl along with the distended stomachs of
hunger, when girls are sold for a dollar to the
keepers of gay houses outside the Chien Men,
and when babies die at the dry breasts of their
starving mothers. At first they redoubled their
prayers to the little god, spending hard-earned
coppers in buying incense-sticks of scented cedar
wood, so that as many as six at a time slowly
powdered into grey ash in the iron bowl at his
feet. But still the sun blazed down, and the rain
came not, and the crops withered. Then their
prayers changed to protestations. The blue-
coated husbandmen reasoned with him in the
evenings, sitting in the dim room where the
smoke curled up to the painted beams. They
pointed out to him that it was his business to
bring them rain in season, that the corn was wither-
ing and that his people would die ; they had done
their part, tilling and sowing and irrigating ;
now it was his turn, and he was not fulfilling
his duty. The anxious women tottered on their
bound feet into his little courtyard, and, standing
by the fish-shaped gong outside the door, held
up their babies for him to see, and implored
him not to let them starve. His was such a little
task, a mere nothing compared with the loves
and hopes and intrigues which the big Buddha

of the Lama temple and Kwan Yin of the Temple-of-the-Upside-Down-Shadow had to bring to a happy upshot. It was so easy, surely he could not fail to perform it. But still the sun blazed down, and the rain came not, and the crops withered.

At last the villagers lost all patience with the little god. " Of what use," they said, " is a god who does not work for his living ? Day after day we have brought him bean-curd and incense-sticks, and he has taken our gifts, but he has not given us that for which we paid him. No trader outside the Ping Tze Men but would be ashamed so to break an ancient bargain ; and he is a god. Either he is in a bad temper, or else he is stupid and has not understood when we have told him that the sun blazes down and the rain comes not and the crops wither. It's cool in there under the high roof. Let us, therefore, take him and put him out in the sun on the steps by the road-side. Then, perhaps, he will see for himself what the weather is like, and when he feels the heat upon his head perhaps he will understand that we must have rain for the crops." So they took up the little god without ceremony and carried him out of his cool, dark room, heavy with incense smoke, and set him down on the steps of the temple beside the high road, where there was no shade, and the burning sun beat down upon his head.

The little god sat on the step, still smiling the same inscrutable smile. He looked down into the road and watched the long line of passers-by making their dusty way from the city to the Western Hills, and from the Western Hills to the city. Sometimes a train of camels passed him very ragged and shabby, each tied to the one in front, the fierce ones muzzled with a muzzle of rope, and the long-legged baby camels dragging wearily in the rear. They were being driven into the upland plains of Mongolia for the summer, and they swayed their long necks and curled their supercilious lips at the little god as they passed. Sometimes a tiny donkey trotted delicately by, with a fat merchant in a wide hat sitting far back upon its rump and rolling a little with the motion while the donkey-boy prodded it from behind with a stick, uttering harsh cries. Sometimes a ricksha passed, drawn by a copper-headed coolie from whose chest and face the sweat fell in great drops upon the dusty road, and in the ricksha a foreign lady, with white skin and a white dress, turned her blue eyes on the little god from under her sunshade. In the distance he would hear the " creak, creak " of the well-rope, which the old mule dragged round and round in an endless circle, turning the wheel which poured a tiny stream of water into the irrigation ditches. Three little gods sat in a covered shed beside the well and superintended these operations, but they were not in disgrace, for several feet of water still stood in the well, bubbling up from a deep spring which never ran dry ; and so they enjoyed their incense in the pleasant shade.

In front of the temple where the little god sat in the sun, a fruit-seller squatted all day, with peaches and apricots arranged in little pyramids of four upon wide green leaves, and enormous melons with shining rinds. At intervals he sprinkled them with water out of an old brass pot, and a naked baby sat on the ground beside him, agitating a big brown-paper fan to keep the clustering flies off the fruit. All these things, which he had never seen before, the little god observed as he sat in the sun outside his temple. And it was very hot indeed, so hot that the burnished lacquer of his back began to crack in places and his head felt like one of those round balls of clay and powdered charcoal which the villagers used for fuel.

By and by a little boy came out of one of the houses in the village and made his way along the road, carrying with extreme care over his shoulders a cross-bar, on which were hung two kerosene tins. In order to fill his tins with water from the well he had to pass the place where the little god was sitting in the sun, and when he saw the little god he stopped and set down the tins and observed him solemnly. He was a very

H

brown little boy, and there were no clothes on his round, dusty body ; even his head was shaved to keep him cool, save for one wisp of hair, which was plaited so tightly that it stood bolt upright like an exclamation mark in the exact middle of his crown, and round its tip was wound a strand of scarlet wool. Nevertheless, he was a very hot little boy, and when he saw how the little god had been sitting all day in the burning sun he was sorry for him. He knew, of course, that the little god ought to have sent the rain at least three weeks ago ; but he himself did not always do as he ought. He advanced a chubby finger and touched the tip of the little god's head, but he had to draw it away again quickly, for the golden lacquer burnt him. Then he looked quickly behind to see if anyone were watching, but the fruit-seller was talking to a customer, the baby had fallen asleep, and the last voyager had already gone several yards up the road. The little boy ran to the other side of the road and picked up a handful of dry grass, which grew there under a tree. Hastily he plaited it into a tiny mat and put the mat on to the head of the little god. " It will keep off the worst sun," he whispered. " Nevertheless, rain should be sent." And he took up his kerosene tins and trotted quickly away.

The little god sat, and as he sat he must have thought. For slowly there appeared in the sky over the eastern hills a tiny cloud, and the cloud spread and spread, until great rolling masses of grey covered the sky, and lightning flashed between them and thunder roared and down came the rain in torrents upon the plain. The parched land drank it up, and the crops lifted their heads. The irrigation channels ran with it, and in the lanes of the city the ricksha coolies, caught unaware, splashed ankle-deep in water. It washed away the terrible spectre of famine which had skulked through the villages for three weeks before, and the villagers sat in their little huts and laughed and patted each other's shoulders as they listened to the long, musical " drip, drip " of the rain. " Certainly," they said, " our god saw for himself that the sun was too hot." When the storm was over they came and took the little god, all wet and glistening, from the step, and carried him back into his temple, and they gave him two bowls of soaked millet and lighted before him ten sticks of the best incense. And the little god sat in his old place, with the grey smoke curling round him, and the blue and green and golden beams above his head, and he still smiled his inscrutable smile. But the little cap of plaited grass was never found, because the rain washed it away over the edge of the steps and into a puddle by the side of the road, where a passing mule stamped it into the mud.

Extracts from the Minutes of the 22nd Session of the Advisory Committee on Traffic in Opium and other Dangerous Drugs (May 24th–June 12th, 1937).

Mr. Fuller (U.S.A.)
Russell Pasha (Egypt)

*D*R. *HOO CHI-TSAI* (China) made the following statement:

To sum up, I propose to quote yet another independent witness—Dr. Stampar—who was sent to China by the League of Nations and who knows the country very well. On his return from China, Dr. Stampar presented to the Health Committee a striking report (document C.H. 1220) which has been published in the *Bulletin of the Health Organisation*. That report says:

" The success of the opium campaign calls for particular notice. Formerly cultivated extensively, opium is now grown in only a few provinces, and the punctuality with which the suppression programme has been carried out gives confidence that it will be brought to completion. Besides limiting the area cultivating the poppy, the Government is taking more direct measures, compelling all opium addicts to be registered and establishing opium hospitals for their cure. Traders in narcotics have been very severely punished. It must be added, however, that the Government is seriously impeded in its work by the existence of extra-territorial privileges."

Such is the evidence of a person well qualified to express an opinion on what is happening in China. There is no need to explain the significance of the last phrase referring to extra-territorial privileges, which seriously hamper the Chinese Government's action in the matter of drugs. The Committee is aware that smuggling in the East, especially of manufactured drugs, practised by certain foreign nationals who are only too well known to the Committee, is paralysing all the efforts of the Chinese Government. Until that situation is changed, China cannot be freed from the drug scourge. The position from this point of view has undergone no change since the last session of the Committee; it has not improved, in spite of the resolution adopted by the Committee in 1936 to which Mr. Renborg has referred. It can be said without exaggeration that the situation has become worse, and that its world repercussions are becoming increasingly apparent. The statements made in the Egyptian report for 1936 on the world sources of white drugs leave no doubt on the subject. In my view, the Committee will not be doing its duty if it does not give all the attention it deserves to this aspect of the problem, which, as I see it, may be regarded as the key to the whole drug problem.

Mr. FULLER (United States of America) made the following statement:

Before undertaking to speak of the situation in China to-day, I wish to say a word or two of appreciation for the Chinese annual report for 1935, which has been in the hands of the Committee for some time past. Fault may be found with this report, on the grounds of incompleteness and of inaccuracy, but this is true of a great many of the other annual reports which are received from Governments. In contrast to previous Chinese reports, the one for 1935 contains a great deal of definite, concrete information—enough to show the nature of the efforts which the Chinese National Government was, in the year under review, devoting to the campaign against the drug evil. And I am informed that a supplementary report will be submitted in respect of 1935 to fill certain gaps in the report already received. I think that the members of the Committee will agree with me that the Chinese annual report for 1935 is unquestionably the best which the Chinese Government has yet presented.

Turning now to the situation in China as it was in 1936 and as it is to-day; China being far and away the largest single producer of raw opium in the world, it would seem logical to consider first : developments in respect of the production of raw opium ; second : the situation in respect of illicit imports ; third : the situation in respect of illicit export ; and lastly : developments in respect of illicit manufacture.

As to the production of raw opium, the information which we have received in my country indicates that, in the provinces of China[1] where there is no Japanese influence, a sincere effort has been made to reduce the production of raw opium and that this effort has met with surprising success. The Committee will recall that, in China south of the Great Wall, the principal producing provinces have for years been Yunnan, Szechuan, and Kweichow. It will recall that, for years past, the production of Yunnan has been estimated at 4500 tons per annum, that of Szechuan at a similar figure and that of Kweichow as usually around 400 tons.

I am happy to say that the information which has reached me indicates that in the three provinces referred to (and they represent most of the production south of the Great Wall), the restrictive measures enforced by the Chinese Government are now commencing to have a noticeable

[1] The reader who is unused to the phraseology of League of Nations documents should bear in mind that the Japanese protectorate of the so called 'Manchukuo' is not recognised by the League, and in consequence the term 'China' here includes 'Manchukuo,' Jehol and northern Chahar.—ED.

effect. The production for the crop year 1936/37 is estimated to have been reduced in Yunnan by about 50 per cent and in Szechuan by about the same proportion, till it now rests at about a half of the usual output.

When we come, however, to the provinces under Japanese control or influence, we find a very different state of affairs. In the three north-eastern provinces—that is to say, Manchuria—we find that the area designated by the regime now functioning in that region for lawful opium-poppy cultivation in 1937 was 156,061 acres, as compared to 133,333 acres in 1936, an increase of 17 per cent; and that unlawful cultivation had reached a point such that the regime referred to found it necessary, on February 6th, 1937, to issue a public warning to unlicensed cultivators. The anticipated gross revenue from Government opium sales in Manchuria in 1937 is estimated at a figure over 28 per cent greater than the gross revenue realised in 1936. As interest in the welfare of the people seems inconsistent with a policy of selling them more opium, one is necessarily led to see in this drive against illicit poppy growing nothing more than an effort to destroy business competition.

Last year[1] I said to the Committee: " Where

[1] See Minutes of the Twenty-first Session of the Committee, p. 66.

Japanese influence advances in the Far East, what goes with it? Drug traffic." This continues to be the case.

The developments of the past year in the province of Chahar afford a striking illustration. When the military forces of the regime now functioning in Manchuria and Jehol occupied northern Chahar, there immediately resulted a forced increase in the area sown to poppy and in opium production; and morphine factories were at once started in Chahar by Japanese. One was started at Kalgan and later moved to Changpeh, where it would not be so conspicuous. Another is at Kalgan. Both use local and Jehol opium. The former is reported to employ 342 persons. The latter is reported to employ 170 workers and to have an output of 50 kilogrammes of heroin daily or some fifteen times the world's legitimate needs.

As for Inner Mongolia, the following excerpt from the *New York Times* of November 17th, 1936, would appear to call for explanation:

" SHANGHAI,
" *November 16th*, 1936.

" The critical Suiyuan province situation, made obscure by many contradictory reports, was clarified this evening by Major-General Seiichi Kita, Japanese Military Attaché in Shanghai, when he explained his country's participation in this curious Inner Mongolian crisis. He said:
" ' In order to offset Outer Mongolia's highly

mechanised army, which is equipped by Russia, we have assisted the Inner Mongolians by selling them planes.' He continued : ' Reports that these Mongols are too poor to buy tanks, armoured cars and munitions are untrue, for they have assets such as a vast opium harvest. We have been paid in kind.' "

Turning now to the question of illicit import into China, the Committee will recall that a great deal has been said, and continues to be said, about the illicit import into China of both raw opium and manufactured drugs. Owing, however, to loose terminology, much of this talk has been misleading. Drugs brought into China from the Kwantung Leased Territory may properly be regarded as imports, but to describe as importations drugs brought into China south of the Wall from China north of the Wall is a misnomer. That is illicit movement within the country and cannot properly be described as import.

Movement of manufactured drugs from Europe to China appears to have ceased entirely in the past three years, the current of illicit traffic having set in the opposite direction. According to reliable information, illicit import into China is now limited to raw Iranian opium from Iran and from Macao, to morphine and heroin from Dairen in the Kwantung Leased Territory, to comparatively small quantities of cocaine from Formosa and Japan and to raw opium from Chosen.

The import into China of raw opium of any origin whatever is forbidden by law. Nevertheless, reliable information is to the effect that 500 chests, or 36,000 kilogrammes, of raw Iranian opium were shipped from Iran to China in the Iranian year 1935/36 and 700 chests, or 51,000 kilogrammes in the Iranian year 1936/37. Contrary to the terms of the drug Conventions, an ever-increasing flood of Iranian opium continues to be imported into Manchuria for use in the manufacture of morphine and heroin, at least forty to fifty tons a year, sufficient for the manufacture of four or five times the world's annual needs of heroin for medical and scientific purposes. The annual report of Macao for 1934 indicated the export from that colony of raw Iranian opium in huge quantities. Subsequent reports of seizures indicate that illicit export from Macao to neighbouring territory continues.

It was reported that, in April, 1936, some 17 tons of Yunnan opium were despatched in a single lot from Yunnanfu by railway across Indo-China to Haiphong and thence by steamer to Kwangchow-Wan (the French leased territory in South China). I am now informed that this lot of opium was almost all transhipped at sea and conveyed for distribution to the Chinese coast near the Canton delta, a small quantity only being delivered at Kwangchow-Wan. Perhaps the French representative or the Chinese representative could give the Committee further information concerning this transaction.

Further, with regard to the smuggling of raw opium into China north of the Great Wall, may be mentioned the movement of raw opium from Chosen to Manchuria. On February 2nd of the current year, Director Munesue, of the Monopoly Bureau of the Government-General of Chosen, was reported in the *Keijo Nippo* (Japanese language organ of the Government-General of Chosen) as having, on February 1st, 1937, made the following statement to the Press :

" About 41,335 lb. of opium have been exported annually to Manchuria. At a conference of departmental opium secretaries in Tokio, it was recently decided to increase this volume pursuant to demands from Manchuria as well as to demands for increased cultivation of poppies in North and South Kankyo provinces.

" In February or March I plan to visit Manchuria to conclude a contract to this end.

" Present compensation to poppy growers is about 120 yen per *kwan* (8,267 lb.). If production is increased from 7,000 *kwan* (57,870 lb.) to 10,000 *kwan* (82,670 lb.), poppy growers will receive more than 1,000,000 yen."

In an official Press release of February 20th, 1937, the Monopoly Bureau of the Government General of Chosen announced a three-year programme of extension of poppy growing, which embodied the following features :

" *Poppy cultivation* : added area of 2,457 acres in Keiki, South Kankyo and Kogen provinces to be developed ; 492 acres in 1937, 1,228 acres in 1938, and 737 acres in 1939.

" *Opium manufacturers' guilds* to be established, to be provided with Government subsidies and be made responsible to the Monopoly Bureau authorities for direction of poppy growing, manufacture and delivery of crude opium, and advancement of loans to poppy growers."

Of possible significance in its relation to the whole problem of increased opium production in Chosen, and the ease with which that drug may be obtained in Chosen, is a Press item of February 24th, 1937, reporting the arrest for opium addiction of a twenty-two-year-old Japanese college student. Efforts to eradicate narcotic addiction in Chosen continue unabated, and the increased opium production referred to is frankly designed for export to Manchuria.

The matter of illicit export from China received extended consideration in the Sub-Committee on Seizures and is discussed in that Sub-Committee's report. With regard to manufactured derivatives of opium, which formerly moved from Europe to China, the current has reversed itself and the movement of such drugs is now from China and Dairen to North America, to Egypt, and to Europe. As of possible interest to the Committee, however, and as illustrating the constant improvement which smugglers

are making in their methods, I am handing
over to the Secretariat a photograph of a packet
of pressed heroin which is reported to be openly
on sale at Tientsin and which is exported
from there to other parts of China, including
Shanghai, by Japanese and Koreans who use
the railway as a means of transportation.
These packets of pressed heroin look exactly
like a cake of packed soap. Each packet
weighs 132 grammes, measures $3\frac{1}{4} \times 2 \times 1\frac{1}{4}$ inches
and costs in Tientsin 37.50 yen per packet. One
side of the cover looks exactly like the photograph[1] while on the other side there is a replica
of a sail-boat surrounded by a fancy frame.
On the narrow sides of the packet, there is an
inscription in Chinese reading : " Beware of
Imitations." Both ends of the packet are sealed
with pieces of paper on which is printed an anchor
with the figures " 235." A piece of string is run
through these pieces of paper and sealed with a
lead plumb. The lead plumb also has an anchor
stamped on one side and the figures " 235 "
on the reverse side. Such packets are mostly
used for local sale. For export, a special packet
is prepared consisting of four similar cases
weighing altogether 569 grammes.

Turning now to the situation in respect of
illicit manufacture, information available to the
American authorities indicates that, while, in a

[1] Kept in the archives of the Secretariat.

few of the provinces south of the Great Wall, some progress was achieved in 1936 in suppression of such manufacture, the manufacture of black base and other opium derivatives continued unabated in all regions under Japanese control or influence, notably in Manchuria and Jehol and in the province of Fukien, and also in certain regions in China to which neither Japanese nor other foreign influence extends.

Fukien Province, where Japanese influence is apparent, using as a raw material principally raw Iranian opium, apparently continues to be the seat of a flourishing heroin manufacture.

The province of Hopei, in which Peiping, Tientsin, and the so-called demilitarised zone are located, has become the seat of the world's most extensive manufacture of illicit heroin. The conditions in Peiping, Tientsin, and Eastern Hopei are appalling and beyond description. In Hopei the traffic is engineered and controlled by Japanese and Koreans, but it should be noted that Szechuan, Kansu, and other outlying provinces which are remote from foreign influence continue to turn out black base and other opium derivatives.

The Committee may be interested to know that, in the summer of 1936, an enterprising dealer in opium at Peiping instituted an advertising campaign, through the mails, to dispose of his opium, as a result of which a number of highly placed and eminently respectable foreigners in that city received circulars in Chinese, a translation of which reads as follows :

" Sir,

" I have been deeply addicted to opium for more than ten years, and have hitherto purchased from smugglers the native opium which I required. The quality was not pure or good, and the price was also very high. Yesterday, through the introduction of my friend, I purchased from the Li K'ang Native Opium Wholesaler 5 oz. of Jehol opium of special grade bearing tax stamps. When I smoked that opium after preparation, I found that the smell was good and that the effect was great. The selling price is 3 dollars only per ounce. Furthermore, there are the first grade which costs 2.80 dollars ; second grade, 2.60 dollars ; third grade, 2.30 dollars ; and Liangchow, 1.90 dollar. All grades bear tax stamps. If you purchase 100 oz. or more, there will be a rebate of 10 cents. It is indeed true that the goods are excellent and that the prices are cheap. The goods are really of superior quality.

" The said Li K'ang Opium Wholesaler is located at No. 10, Hsi Tsung Pu Hut'ung, East City, Peiping, and its telephone number is 1593 East Office. The goods will be sent to you upon receipt of your order by telephone. It will do no harm if all my comrades of the same appetite should make a trial, so as to know that I am telling no lie.

" Respectfully yours,

" A Person of the Same Taste."

I am handing over to the Secretariat a photostatic copy of one of these circulars.

Information in the hands of the American authorities fully confirms the evidence of the Chinese seizure reports and the statements made to the Sub-Committee on Illicit Traffic by the Chinese representative to the effect that illicit traffic in manufactured drugs is rapidly extending down the railways from Hopei Province toward the Yangtze River, due to the energetic work of Japanese and Korean pedlars.

Last year I characterised the situation in Manchuria and Jehol, where, as we were informed by the Japanese representative, there is no legislation to control manufacture of, or trade in, opium derivatives, as "terrifying." According to information received, the condition in that area is now almost beyond belief. This is the one region in the world where the governing authority not only makes no effort to prevent the abuse of narcotic drugs, but actually profits by the rapid increase of narcotic addiction.

The degradation of the population of Manchuria through increasing use of opium and its derivatives has actually come to a pass where even Japanese newspapers published in that area have been moved to protest.

Late in January, 1937, there was held in Hsingking, the seat of the central government in Manchuria (formerly known as Changchun), a conference of provincial governors.

After the statements made at that conference of

I

governors, M. T. Kikuchi, the Japanese editor of the *Sheng Ching Shih Pao* (South Manchuria Railway owned Chinese language daily of Mukden), openly criticised the Government's narcotics policy. He charged that (1) the licensed opium retailing system has not checked the spreading use of that drug, (2) large numbers of young people have taken to narcotics, (3) it is inconsistent for the Government to advocate the improvement of public health and yet permit the population to be poisoned by narcotics, (4) opium and its derivatives are a blot on " Manchukuo's " honour. With the permission of the Committee, I will read translations of three courageous articles from M. Kikuchi's newspaper.

[*Sheng Ching Shih Pao*, MUKDEN, MANCHURIA,
January 24th, 1937.]

" *Second Day Conference of Provincial Governors of*
" *Manchukuo.*

" The Conference of Manchukuo provincial governors was opened on January 22nd, 1937. The second day conference started at 10 a.m.

" On the second day questions and answers were freely raised and made by the governors and bureau directors of the Central Government departments. . . . Public health, colonisation and civil engineering matters were discussed. Both the provincial governors and the bureau directors were unanimous in their opinion that the people's health should be improved and that opium can make Manchukuo perish. They further expressed a hope that the

Government will make proper disposal of such matters as a re-examination of the opium policy, evils of opium retail houses, prevention of young people from becoming addicted to narcotics, and an expansion of national hospitals."

*   *   *

[Editorial in *Sheng Ching Shih Pao, January* 27*th,* 1937.]

" *Opium Retailing and Health Preservation.*

" The danger of opium is known by everyone. There has long been talk of racial and national perdition through opium-smoking. After the establishment of Manchukuo, the Government adopted the licensed opium-house system to prohibit opium-smoking gradually, as it was feared that opium addicts of long standing could not stop smoking immediately. Simultaneously, opium addict sanitaria were established in various places for curing the habit and restoring normal health.

" From the time the opium retail system was established, we have written editorials to serve as warnings. Contrary to expectations, after several years of the enforcement of the opium-retail system, none of the opium addicts has stopped smoking and, in addition, a large number of young people have become opium-smokers. It is, therefore, to the point that at the governors' conference there was expressed a desire to re-examine the licensed opium-house question, in order that the people's health may be preserved.

" In recent years the Government has paid careful attention to the health of the people, and has endeavoured to improve it. Yet the adoption of the

licensed opium-house system and the freedom
allowed the people to smoke opium as they please
in licensed opium-houses affects their health far
more than unsanitary conditions. Opium, together
with heroin and morphia, causes many deaths (in
Manchuria).

" It may be said that, since there are opium-addict
sanitaria already established for the treatment of the
public, the Government can do nothing more if the
people themselves take to narcotics like the moths
flying into a flame. We feel, however, that, if a
proper procedure is required for the purchase of
opium and that if the number of licensed opium-
houses is decreased, it may be possible to reduce
the number of opium-smokers. It is, after all, a
shame for any civilised country to permit the open
sale of narcotics. In extenuation, it may be said that
our country adopted the licensed opium-retail
system only as a temporary measure, it having been
decided to reduce annually the opium cultivation
areas. It would seem practicable to designate a
limited number of years for addicts to break off the
habit, if not out of public health considerations, at
least, in order to adhere to the original aim of reduced consumption.

" The provincial governors this time are of the
same opinion as we in regard to the re-examination
of the opium question. That is, the people must
universally be healthy. Then the country and its
race can develop sturdily. The present curious form
of health preservation leaves a blot. Moreover,
the logic of discussing public health and yet allow-
ing the people to be poisoned seems to be inconsistent. The present conditions may be a plan to get
rid of the weak and keep the good. It is, neverthe-

less, a disgraceful reflection on the people that they should continue to take poison like candy, in spite of the existence of opium-addict sanitaria and public-health organisations. Once orders are issued by the Government, none of the addicts will dare disobey them. If opium-smoking is to be controlled only when the situation develops to its worst, then it will be too late.

" It is sometimes said that since opium addicts cannot return to normal health, it would be better to let them live or die as they like. We ask, what harm can there be in strictly prohibiting them to smoke opium ? Those who die due to Government prohibition are a minority. And by such prohibition, the addiction of young people to the drug may be checked. This will naturally greatly preserve the health of the people.

" Some say that opium is a rich source of Government revenue. If it is suddenly cut off, the Government cannot make up the loss. We maintain that the land of Manchukuo is wide and fertile, and that the cultivation of other crops to take the place of opium would compensate for the loss.

" Why leave this shame, making possible the existence in this country of unhealthy people ? We have suggested to the governors' conference a re-examination of the opium-retail question, and although we have not yet heard of the results, it is felt that the Central Government authorities will, for the health of the people, take the matter into deep consideration and make proper disposal of it."

*   *   *

[*Sheng Ching Shih Pao*, MUKDEN, MANCHURIA,
February 18*th*, 1937.]

" *Number of Deaths in Mukden during January due
to Narcotics Poisoning.*

" The number of deaths in the Mukden munici-
pality during January due to narcotics poisoning
has been investigated by the Public Health Section
of the Shenyang Police Bureau and is as follows :

	Morphia		Heroin		Opium		Total
	Men	Women	Men	Women	Men	Women	
Reported by :							
City Police Office	5	1	—	—	—	—	6
East suburb Police Office..................	7	—	1	1	—	—	9
North suburb Police Office..................	1	—	2	—	—	—	3
South market Police Office..................	44	4	27	2	—	—	77
North market Police Office..................	59	—	10	—	1	—	70
Police Office West of railway	6	—	—	—	—	—	6
Total	122	5	40	3	1	—	171

This ends, for the time being, my quotations
from the *Sheng Ching Shih Pao*.

Press reports have stated that, in 1935, in the
principal cities of Manchuria, nearly 6000 persons
died of narcotic addiction without any provision

for their interment. As bearing on this subject, I quote below the statement of an eye-witness who was in Mukden in October, 1936 :

"Adjacent to a rag-pickers' market about a reeking open sewer are some fifty or more hovels inhabited by the lowest type of prostitutes who, in addition to their regular occupation, also openly dispense narcotics. The setting was loathsome to a degree. Demonstrating with peculiar force the relation of cause to effect, there lay on an ash-heap just behind the narcotic brothels seven naked corpses which had evidently been stripped of their rags by fellow-addicts. It is generally stated that this is a daily sight, despite regular removal of the bodies by the Red Swastika Society. There was offered no other explanation than that these dead met their end through narcotics poisoning."

The ash heaps of Mukden and Harbin have become so notorious that M. Kikuchi was moved to write the following editorial, which I quote in translation :

[*Sheng Ching Shih Pao*, MUKDEN, MANCHURIA,
February 18th, 1937.]

"*Many Dead on Kung Fu Shih Ash-Heap.*

"Everyone knows the danger of morphia. There are many people who die from its poison each year. It is lamentable to say that these people, in becoming addicted to morphia, are digging their own graves. The ash-heap at Kung Fu Shih, outside of the large west city gate, is the morphia centre of Mukden. It is general knowledge that almost daily drug-addicts die there.

"It is now learned that at the foot of the ash-heap there were found dead during the several days after the Lunar New Year thirteen young men of about twenty years of age. Their hair was dishevelled and their faces dirty. They could be recognised at a glance as morphia-addicts. Their upper garments and trousers were stripped from their bodies. Some of them were lying on the ground with their faces turned upward ; some with their faces covered ; and some were lying in the gutters. It was a pitiable sight. On the morning of the 16th instant, these dead bodies were still lying at that place.

"It is deeply hoped that the Municipal Government and philanthropic organisations will, at an early date, dress these corpses for burial, so as to show regard for humanity and to improve the appearance of the city."

What has the Government which holds or should hold itself responsible for the welfare of the people of Manchuria done about this ? In the conference of provincial governors no remedial measures are reported to have been advocated. The Government's opium programme for 1937 envisages a 25 per cent increase in sales over 1936. No intention has been exhibited to check the brazen traffic in morphine and heroin. Mr. Chairman, I put it to you that this is a sad but most illuminating example of the results of greed, of large-scale poisoning of one's fellow-man for gain and an example of total disregard of the obligations which any

Government, *de facto* or *de jure*, which hopes to enjoy respect, confidence or recognition, has toward other governments of the world.

Many of those present will recall an occasion, not so very long ago, when in this Committee an *exposé* was made of illicit manufacture which had suddenly sprung up in an alarming manner in a certain country—an occasion when one of our oldest and most respected colleagues said :

" This cancer on the face of Europe must be extirpated."

It was. Now we have another cancer, this time on the face of Asia. It remains to be seen whether those responsible for the ash-heaps of Harbin and Mukden, Tongshan, Tientsin and Peiping will do anything about it before they are overtaken by a retribution which all their ill-gotten gains cannot avert.

RUSSELL PASHA (Egypt) made the following statement :

We have all heard Mr. Fuller's full and authenticated statement on the state of affairs existing in the Japanese-controlled territories north of the Great Wall and in some parts of China proper.

I do not know what impression it has made on members of this Committee who have heard it for the first time. If the result is scepticism or a self-satisfying hope that things are not really as bad as they are painted, all I can tell them is that I, too, have got full and ample reports by eye-witnesses which amply confirm what Mr. Fuller and others have said.

As heroin manufacture and sale constitute apparently a perfectly open and authorised trade in Manchuria and Jehol, it is possible for any intelligent traveller to judge of the enormous proportions at which this trade has now arrived, to see with his own eyes the ghastly effects that it is producing on the population and the menace that it is to the rest of the civilised world.

Without attempting to give you a complete account of the narcotic industry and conditions in Manchuria and Jehol, I will quote you some sentences from reports received :

"In the city of Harbin there are to-day not less than 300 heroin dens without counting those in the city of Foochiatien, which is practically part of Harbin.

"These dens are visited daily by about 50,000 addicts of Chinese, Russian and Japanese nationality.

"Besides these heroin dens, there are in Harbin and Foochiatien 102 authorised opium-saloons which also sell heroin. The number of clients of these dens is about 20 Europeans and 300 Chinese for each den daily.

"Practically one-quarter of the one million inhabitants of these two cities are addicts. . . .[1]

"During the very severe Harbin winters many

[1] One sentence omitted at the speaker's request.—ED.

addicts die in the street : their corpses are left for days in the streets, as nobody bothers to take them away; even the dogs sometimes will not eat them.

"The supply of drugs is not manufactured in Harbin itself. It comes entirely from the Japanese Concession in Mukden and from Dairen. It is from Dairen that thousands of letters containing drugs are posted to the United States, Egypt and elsewhere.

"The Podol district of Foochiatien is full of heroin dens ; there must certainly be a thousand, all for the poorest class of the population ; near to the district is a bazaar where second-hand and stolen goods are sold in exchange for heroin. . . . In this district, corpses of addicts are found daily ; other addicts are paid ten yen to take away a corpse and bury it. . . . No formalities.

"Peasants arrive daily at Foochiatien to sell their farm produce; they are paid in heroin, and addiction is rife among them ; they are pawning their horses, their cattle and even their houses for heroin, till they become completely beggared and their lands are taken over by the opium Monopoly."

These quotations could be continued indefinitely. As you will see from them, conditions in these parts are staggering to the mind of any man who has a sense of decency and pity towards his fellow-men.

The evil is, however, so general and spread over such enormous territories that it is difficult for us, living our comfortable lives, to concentrate our thoughts and actually visualise what these things mean.

Mr. Fuller has described, and other eye-witnesses have written, accounts of conditions in the Japanese concession of Tientsin; one such eye-witness has described the situation to me as follows:

"The Japanese Concession in Tientsin is now known as the nerve centre of heroin manufacture and addiction of the world. The number of opium and heroin dens which go under the names of Yang Hang or foreign firms, number well over a thousand; in addition, there are hundreds of hotels, shops and other establishments where white drugs are openly sold. Not less than 200 heroin factories are scattered over the Japanese Concession, which is only about four square miles in size. Over 1500 Japanese experts and 10,000 Chinese workmen are engaged in the manufacture of heroin. As the business is extremely profitable and the supply of raw material abundant, new factories are starting daily; the factories are working perfectly openly.

"Hashidaté Street is the heart of the heroin belt in China. There are in it more than fifty shops, and heroin can be purchased freely in all of them. The heroin is of excellent quality, without adulteration and cheap, the gramme in retail selling for 1 Chinese dollar, while the wholesale price is 500 Chinese dollars (about £45) the kilogramme."

(Russell Pasha added, for purposes of comparison, that the price of one kilogramme of pure heroin in Cairo at the present time would be from £500 to £600.)

"Every night we can see coolies and merchants

walking about the streets offering heroin for sale. After the famous Manchuria and Jehol dens and factories, the Japanese Concession in Tientsin has become the heroin centre of China proper and of the world, and it is from here that not only the Chinese race but all other countries of the world are being weakened and debauched.

" To the traffickers, of course, the foreign, and especially the American, trade is the most profitable. Most of the narcotics, intercepted abroad, bear a mark of Chinese origin. The reason for this is simple : Japanese laws do not allow export of drugs to foreign countries from Japan or via Japan ; it becomes necessary, therefore, to ship the goods to foreign ports via Shanghai and in some cases direct from Tientsin.

" I have made a very careful calculation and estimate that 500 kilogrammes or more of heroin are shipped weekly direct from Tientsin. This quantity is divided roughly as follows : 60 per cent direct to the United States, 30 per cent to the United States via European countries and ports, and the remaining 10 per cent to other countries, including Egypt.

" We should not be far short of the mark if we said that 90 per cent of all the illicit white drugs of the world are of Japanese origin, manufactured in the Japanese Concession of Tientsin, around Tientsin, in or around Dairen or in other cities of Manchuria, Jehol and China, and this always by Japanese or under Japanese supervision. As for the conditions in the dens of the Japanese Concession, words fail when I attempt to describe the revolting and terrible conditions. The dens are dark, the filth is revolting and the scenes ghastly even to a hardened person like myself; in the brothels adjoining the dens, young girls give filthy exhibitions for the sake of a shot of heroin; Chinese, Russians, foreigners, lie about on the dirty wooden boards, as also children of two and three years of age, already idiot drug addicts, with swollen heads and thin, transparent bodies.

" In the first room of the dens, Korean women [never themselves addicts] are busy at their tasks mixing the heroin with adulterants. A small dose costs 10 cents, 50 cents for a dose of a better quality or for an injection of morphine. The injections are done with dirty syringes, often home-made; the needles are never washed, disinfected or changed, and syphilis is freely spread by the needles from one addict to another. I have seen addicts with whole parts of their chests just a mass of decomposed and gangrenous flesh, with holes in their bodies that you could put your whole fist into, and it is into these putrefying, barely living corpses that the needles of dope are alternately pushed."

I will quote no more.

Mr. Chairman, these conditions exist to-day. There is no getting away from facts. Can we not somehow stir the consciences of those responsible to wipe out this blot on civilisation? This morning my Cairo post informs me that a month ago not less than fifty heroin factories in the Japanese Concession of Tientsin have moved to Tangshan, some two hours distant by train, and that most of the others are to follow.

Let us hope that this is not merely a change of scene, but that it denotes the intention of the authorities to begin the definite closing-down of these sinks of iniquity and depravity.

M. Yokoyama (Japan) said that with regard to North China, the Japanese authorities intended, as soon as possible, to ratify the 1936 Convention. Meanwhile, patience was necessary, but M. Yokoyama could assure the Committee that there could be no doubt as to Japan's good faith.

The position in Tientsin had been described. Everyone wished to improve, as quickly as possible, the deplorable state of affairs existing there. In order to do so, however, the cause and not the effect must be attacked. The reason for that situation was chiefly political and geographical. Tientsin was situated between two parts of China with entirely different legislations. In South China, there was a total prohibition of narcotic drugs which did not exist in " Manchukuo." Tientsin was the weak spot in the organism and therefore the most readily attacked by the germ of drug addiction. Malefactors existed in Japan as elsewhere, and when the situation was made too difficult for them in Japan they naturally went elsewhere. The Japanese authorities were doing their best, but patience was necessary.

It had also been alleged that the increase in the illicit traffic in China coincided with the Japanese advance. Such a statement was at least exaggerated, if not wholly inaccurate. If it were true, it might be said that there were other influences than Japanese at work. In some cases it might be a mere coincidence. The Japanese army went wherever military defence was necessary ; national defence naturally took precedence over all other problems. Narcotic drugs were a great danger, but the danger of bombs and machine-guns was greater still. The military authorities devoted as much time as they could to the suppression of the illicit traffic.

M. Yokoyama therefore asked that the some-what annoying bluntness of the allegations made should be modified.

M. Yokoyama's feelings on the matter were divided. He had a dual personality : as an idealist he would like to have action taken im-mediately, even if it necessitated sending sheaves of telegrams to his Government, but as a practical man he realised that the difficulties were so great, the countries so far away, that no formal promise could be made. Japan laid too great store on her national honour to make promises that could not be carried out.

CHINA'S NEW UNITY

Sir Arthur Salter

I HAVE twice visited China to advise the Nanking Government on its reconstruction programme. The first occasion was in 1931, the second after an interval of three years. My impressions were that the difficulties facing the Chinese Government were greater than we, in the West, made allowance for ; that nevertheless the reconstruction programme was more ambitious than we had realised ; that the programme was no mere paper one and that, in spite of many disappointments, it stood a fair chance of being brought to a successful completion. Especially the difference between what I saw in 1931 and in 1934 brought home to me the relative speed with which the transformation was being carried out.

Though China some years ago became a byword for disorder, few people in England realise how calamitous was the state of the country when the Kuomintang Government came into power. Not only had China been wasted by fifteen years of civil war, but the age-old political structure had collapsed, and had to be built anew, for the most part on a new pattern.

The material destruction, taken by itself, would have sufficiently taxed the Government. The Chinese, owing to the over-population of the more fertile areas, are accustomed, even in years of greatest prosperity, to a very slender margin between income and subsistence level; and in times of strain, political or economic, income quickly falls below the margin. The disturbances following the revolution of 1911 caused distress such as we in Europe can hardly imagine: for any parallel here we should have to go back to the Thirty Years War, or the Tartar invasions. The descriptions of desolation in the Old Testament would not have been inappropriate for the conditions in many of the provinces.

> " The cities shall be wasted without inhabitants, and the houses without men, and the land shall be utterly desolate, and the Lord shall have removed men far away and there shall be a great forsaking in the midst of the land."

Capital had been withdrawn from the countryside, and the peasantry either continued their farming on a primitive and hardly supportable level or else abandoned their fields. Areas as large as English counties were allowed to lie waste. The dykes, on which the safety of millions depend, fell into disrepair; the floods of recent years, technically an act of God, were made

possible by the negligence of men. Rail construction, so promising at the beginning of the
century, had ceased; railways, in fact, proved
a curse to the peasantry, since those living in
the railway zone were more easily fleeced by the
military. An especially impressive sign of the
economic collapse was the destruction for fire-
wood of the mulberry groves, the capital equip-
ment upon which was based China's most
characteristic industry.

The political crisis was a still graver one. The
system of government to which China had for
centuries been accustomed—under which China
had developed one of the greatest, and most
pacific, civilisations the world has yet known—
was a federation of villages and clans, each of
which, in fact if not in theory, was to a great
extent free to control its own affairs. The
Central Government defended the frontiers and
performed the national religious rites; its functions, beyond this, were very limited. What
held the nation together, what caused the local
magistrates to deal leniently with the people, and
the people to live peaceably with one another,
was the Confucian system of ethics, a code of
behaviour universally reverenced and to a surprising degree actually practised. In the early
years of the century this system of government
collapsed. On the one hand, as the result partly
of an economic crisis, due to the impact of the

economy of the West, partly of a crisis of over-population, the peasantry became so impover-ished that banditry increased to an alarming extent. On the other hand, the Central Government, faced with new problems, national and international, by the changing social and economic circumstances, failed to develop the powers needed to cope with them. Thus it forfeited the confidence of the nation : it became, in the words of the famous Prime Minister, Li Hung-chang, a " paper tiger," impressive to look at, but without force. Rejecting, after the brief liberal phase of 1898, all proposals for thorough-going reform, it antagonised the intelligentsia : who devoted themselves not to the construction of a new political system in China, but to the destruction of the old. In 1911 the Government fell ; and to take its place there was neither a resolute political party nor a bureaucracy able to function as a united whole nor an army able to command the obedience of its local generals.

The result—in the circumstances an almost inevitable result—was a period of anarchy. The bourgeoisie, who had expected to set up in China a replica of the Western parliamentary system, quickly learned that in politics *ex nihilo nihil fit.* Power passed into the hands of local military leaders ; as had happened in Europe in the Dark Ages when the Roman Government disintegrated. The rule of law virtually ceased ; and the local institutions took the contagion of the central ones and fell into decay. But whereas in Europe the Dark Ages lasted for centuries, in China the period of worst confusion was over—for reasons resulting from the international as well as the domestic situation—in less than two decades. The establishment of the Nanking Government marked a new stage in Chinese history, the attempt at reconstruction.

There is not room here to describe in detail the Government's achievements; and to catalogue them in outline would convey little. But mention of a few facts and factors may serve to give an impressionist picture of the state of affairs just before the Japanese invasion.

The country had become more orderly and was safer for the private citizen than it had been for many years. It was more unified. The political system held out greater prospects of stability. The officials had become more conscientious and more competent; and the Government had created at least the framework of an up-to-date administrative machine. In Chinese politics of the past ten years it is possible to see, for all their tortuousness, some kind of consistent course and development. The revolution of 1911 split Chinese society into a multitude of groups and parties, no one of which alone could become predominant; the art of Chiang Kai-shek was to create a coalition—the composition of which he has varied according to circumstances—which has commanded sufficient obedience to make possible the resumption, at least partial, of National Government. The coalition began as a bloc of the intelligentsia (radical and moderate), the bankers and business interests, groups of the rural gentry, and some of the feudal war lords; it was contracted, after the setting up of the Government in Nanking, by the exclusion of the radical wing; and by the expulsion a little later —often overlooked by radical critics of Nanking —of its more feudal and reactionary members. The success of the Government bloc both attracted to its support all the moderate, " centre " elements in China : and simultaneously moderated the zeal of some of the more radical factions. For the Nanking system is a latitudinarian one : within it most of the factions can, by give and take, realise at least some of their pet projects : out-and-out opposition condemns them to political sterility. It is a system which has, of course, many defects. It requires the nicest manipulation; the attempt by Chiang Kai-shek, only recently abandoned, to give to the parties of the Right a somewhat disproportionate weight in the coalition was probably an error of judgment, dearly paid for by the so-called Communist wars. It is not (as yet) a democratic system. It is irritating to the constitutional lawyer, by reason of its vagueness and the indeterminate nature of its institutions. Nevertheless, it is probably, in the very complex circumstances of China, the only system practicable in the circumstances of recent years : the system rousing least opposition, involving least civil war, and holding out the best prospects of development. Justifying its informality Chinese often compare their system of government to the British constitution. Mr. Hughes, in his latest book, describes their attitude:

" The Nationalist Revolution brought a cons sciousness of past mistakes, of which the chief one is felt to be too much attention to democratic form-and failure to work for the democratic spirit. Hence the willingness to scrap the forms of democracy and to have a one-party government. The aim is to foster a spirit and let forms be discovered later. . . . The solutions, from the point of view of administrative machinery, may be anything."

The improvement of the economic situation can be much more easily assessed. Perhaps the outstanding feature has been the reform and unification of the currency. The value to a country, both political and economic, of a stable, single currency hardly needs pointing out. When I first visited China the country was nominally on a silver standard ; but in addition to silver dollars there existed the tael, a standard of value which was in silver but was not coined ; the weight of the tael varied in different parts of the country ; there existed also many paper currencies,

issued by different banks and local authorities,
and at widely varying rates of depreciation;
and finally the peasantry, three-quarters of the
entire population, made most of their transactions
not in silver, but in copper, the value of which,
in terms of silver, fluctuated widely both season-
ally and over the long period. I formed the
opinion that, in view of the fluctuations to
which silver was subjected it would be an
advantage for the dollar to be linked to gold or
to one of the major world currencies. But
so great were the impediments to this reform
that I expected many years to pass before its
completion. By 1937, only six years after,
China had a unified currency linked in practice
to sterling: and strong enough to withstand for
a considerable time the strain of war without depreciation. The reform of the financial
administration and banking system and renewal
of debt service; the revival of railway construction, following the reorganisation of the railway
debt; the building, in less than ten years, of
more than 100,000 kilometres of motor roads
are achievements which, by creating a new
economic framework, seemed, before the out-
break of the present war, to have prepared
the way for rapid economic development,
both in the ports and the interior, and to
have at last made possible the renewal on a
large scale of financial co-operation between

China and the West. Nor, in its absorption with
these central problems, had the Government
neglected the peasantry and their needs. The
National Economic Council was establishing, in
association with the provincial Governments, a
chain of welfare centres in the country districts.
These centres provided free education, both for
adults and children ; dispensed medical services ;
distributed better seeds to the farmers and advised
them on better agricultural methods ; and
attempted, by improving the marketing system,
to revive the domestic industries.

Government commissions have been attempting to improve, on a national scale, all branches
of the silk, cotton, and tea industries. Great
stress has been laid on the spread of the co-operative movement, the view being that if the farmer
can get cheap credit and fair treatment in the
marketing of his produce many of his difficulties
will be solved. The spread of the co-operative
movement is indeed a remarkable phenomena
in modern China. In the years 1932–5 the
number of societies increased from 5000 to over
15,000. The difficulty, mét with not only in this,
but in all lines of reconstructive activity, of a
lack of trained technical personnel was being over-
come by the provision of training courses in the
Universities and middle schools ; the shortage of
technical staff was for the time the main limiting
factor to a rapid expansion of the social services.

The extent of China's reconstruction programme can be, and often has been, exaggerated
—sometimes as the result of the state of mind
which finds it wonderful that Chinese can perform
the same mechanical feats as Westerners. But
more often it is underrated; it is well to have
a just estimate of it in calculating the possi-
bilities of a prolonged resistance. The new
roads, as much as the valour of the soldiers,
made possible the defence of Shanghai. In some
measure the reconstruction programme has perhaps been responsible for the war itself. For,
of the mixed motives which led Japan to take
decisive action, one was probably the desire to
strike before China had had time to improve
still further its defence. Japan's relation to
China is not unlike that of Macbeth to Banquo.
Even if the worst should befall China, and Japan
should succeed in dominating the Far East for a
generation, Japan would still, looking towards
its neighbour, feel that that fate which gave it
priority in its industrialisation had given it also
but a limited time in which to enjoy its supremacy.

> *" Upon my head it placed a fruitless crown*
> *And put a barren sceptre in my gripe,*
> *Thence to be wrencht with an unlineal hand."*

But however great our hopes, or confident
expectations, for China's ultimate salvation, we
cannot be the less keenly alive to the horror of
what is taking place, or to the at least partial

responsibility of the Western world for the tragedy. After a quarter-century of misery such as I outlined above, China, as the result of its own exertions, and against the expectations of many observers, had successfully laid at least the foundation of a modern State system. It must now, whatever the result of the war, be a long time before that foundation is built upon; indeed, if the Japanese are victorious the foundation may be deliberately demolished. Of the period of anarchy following the revolution of 1911—the collapse of the age-old, pacific, self-ordering society of China—the West was, as we have seen above, consciously or unconsciously in great part the cause. The Christian missions, the Universities and Western learning, Western political thought, Western industrial and commercial technique, whether or not they may in the long run prove beneficial to China, operated at first to destroy the old regime. This is now fairly generally recognised; and candid study must bring home to us that the responsibility of the West for this second tribulation which has now befallen China is, though less direct, hardly less great; though, of course, it is entirely unintentional. Japan is capable of aggression against China only because it adopted (more quickly than China) the arms, and industrial and administrative technique of the West; and the moral outlook of the West of the late nineteenth century. The civilisation of which the U.S.A. and Great Britain are now the greatest representatives has over the last century broken the great pacific civilisation of the East. For Japan the tragedy is the debasement of its national life and lowering of its morale; for China material and political ruin and the frustration of the most devoted efforts to build its civilisation anew.

CHUANG TZU AND HUI TZU: INTUITION VERSUS INTELLECT

Arthur Waley

EVERYONE has heard of Lao Tzu, but very little is known to the average English reader about that other great collection of Taoist sayings, *Chuang Tzu*, despite the existence of several translations, both partial and complete. The book is indeed a rather long one; but that can scarcely be the reason of its unpopularity; for English readers are by no means averse to long books. The reason is, I think, that the text is very corrupt. The commentators attempt to force a meaning out of passages that are in fact meaningless as they stand, and translators follow suit. Moreover, the text is in great disorder, so that passages which belong together and even different parts of the same sentence have become widely separated. The only way to understand the intelligible portions of the book is to read them in connection with other similar passages. A great deal can be learned by comparing all the passages in which, for example, the qualities of various ideal beings (the Purified Man, the Sage, the Man who has Arrived) are defined. Or again, one can get a much clearer idea of what the various interlocutors in the book really stand for by comparing the passages in which they figure. Here I have arranged in a convenient order the passages in which Chuang Tzu and Hui Tzu appear, omitting those which are either too fragmentary or textually corrupt beyond possibility of certain emendation.

It will be seen that Hui Tzu figures as a logician, an intellectualist, an analyst ; Chuang Tzu as an intuitive, a mystic, a synthetist. To typify Hui Tzu's logical enquiries, Chuang Tzu speaks of the " hard " and the " white." Our eye tells us that a stone is white, our fingers tell us that it is hard. Is what our eye tells us the truth or only part of the truth ? . . . And so on. It must have been with such speculations that Hui Tzu was occupied, but we only possess a fragment of a treatise on this subject by a follower of Hui Tzu ; it does not follow that Hui Tzu himself handled the theme in the same way. Moreover, this fragment is, to me at any rate, barely intelligible, so that we must be content to accept " the hard and the white " merely as the label of Hui Tzu's mysterious dialectic. Those who compare my translation with the original will see that I have made a certain number of small emendations. These I hope to discuss in a future publication.

Hui Tzu said to Chuang Tzu, "Your teachings are of no practical use." Chuang Tzu said, "Only those who already know the value of the useless can be talked to about the useful. This earth we walk upon is of vast extent, yet in order to walk a man uses no more of it than the soles of his two feet will cover. But suppose one cut away the ground round his feet till one had reached the Yellow Springs ?[1] Would his patches of ground still be of any use to him for walking ? " Hui Tzu said, "They would be of no use." Chuang Tzu said, "So then the usefulness of the useless is evident."

Hui Tzu recited to Chuang Tzu the rhyme,

> *I have got a big tree*
> *That men call the* chü.
> *Its trunk is knotted and gnarled,*
> *And cannot be fitted to plumb-line and ink ;*
> *Its branches are bent and twisted,*
> *And cannot be fitted to compass or square.*
> *It stands by the road-side,*
> *And no carpenter will look at it.*

"Your doctrines," said Hui Tzu, "are grandiose, but useless, and that is why no one accepts them." Chuang Tzu said, "Can it be that you have never seen the pole-cat, how it crouches waiting for the mouse, ready at a moment to leap this way or that, high or low, till one day it lands plump on the spring of a trap and dies in the snare ? Again there is the yak, ' huge as a cloud that covers the

[1] The World of the dead.

sky.' It can maintain its huge bulk and yet would be quite incapable of catching a mouse. . . . As for you and the big tree which you are at a loss how to use, why do you not plant it in the realm of Nothing Whatever, in the wilds of the Unpastured Desert, and aimlessly tread the Path of Inaction by its side, or vacantly lie dreaming beneath it ?

> *What does not invite the axe*
> *No creature will harm.*
> *What cannot be used*
> *No troubles will befall.*"

Hui Tzu said to Chuang Tzu, " The king of Wei gave me the seed of one of his huge gourds. I planted it and it bore a gourd so enormous that if I had filled it with water or broth it would have taken several men to lift it, while if I had split it into halves and made ladles out of it they would have been so flat that no liquid would have lain in them. No one could deny that it was magnificently large ; but I was unable to find any use for it, and in the end I smashed it up and threw it away." Chuang Tzu said, " I have noticed before that you are not very clever at turning large things to account. There was once a family in Sung that possessed a secret drug which had enabled its members for generations past to steep silk floss without getting chapped hands. A stranger hearing of it offered to buy the recipe for a hundred pieces of gold. The head of the family pointed out to his kinsmen that if all the money that the family had made in successive generations through the use of the drug were added together it would not come to more than one or two pieces of gold, and that a hundred pieces would amply repay them for parting with their secret. The stranger carried off the recipe and spoke of it to the king of Wu, whose country was being harried by the battle-ships of Yüeh. The stranger was put in command of the Wu fleet and so efficacious was the remedy that despite the bitter cold (for it was a winter's day), the fingers of the Wu sailors never once grew chapped or numbed, and the fleet of Yüeh was entirely destroyed. The land of Yüeh was divided and the stranger rewarded with a fief. The sole property of the drug was that it prevented hands from getting chapped. Yet so much depends on the user that, if it had stayed with the man of Sung, it would never have done more than help him to steep floss; while no sooner had it passed into the stranger's possession than it gained him a fief. As for you and your large gourd, why did you not tie it as a buoy at your wrist and, borne up by it in the waters, float to your heart's content amid the streams and inland seas? Instead, you grumble about its gigantic dimensions and say that ladles made from it would hold nothing; the reason being, I fear, that your own thoughts have not learnt to run beyond the commonplace."

L

Hui Tzu said to Chuang Tzu, "Can a man really become passionless?" Chuang Tzu said, "He can." Hui Tzu said, "A man without passions cannot be called a man." Chuang Tzu said, "'Tao gave him substance, Heaven gave him form'; how is it possible not to call him a man?" Hui Tzu said, "I would rather say, Granted that he is still a man, how is it possible for him to be passionless?" Chuang Tzu said, "You do not understand what I mean when I say 'passionless.' When I say 'passionless' I mean that a man does not let love or hate do him damage within, that he falls in with the way in which things happen of themselves, and does not exploit life." Hui Tzu said, "If he does not exploit life, what is the use of his having a body?" Chuang Tzu said:

> "*Tao gave him substance,*
> *Heaven gave him form;*
> *Let him not by love or hate*
> *Bring this gift to harm.*

Yet here are you

> *Destroying your soul,*
> *Wearying your spirit,*
> *Propped against a pile of books you drone,*
> *Leaning against your zithern you doze.*
> *Heaven made you sound and whole;*
> *Yet all your song is hard and white.*"

When Chuang Tzu's wife died, Hui Tzu came to the house to join in the rites of mourning.

To his surprise he found Chuang Tzu sitting
with an inverted bowl on his knees, drumming
upon it and singing a song.[1] " After all," said
Hui Tzu, " she lived with you, brought up your
children, grew old along with you. That you
should not mourn for her is bad enough ; but
to let your friends find you drumming and singing
—that is really going too far ! " " You misjudge
me," said Chuang Tzu. " When she died, I was
in despair, as any man well might be. But soon,
pondering on what had happened, I told myself
that in death no strange new fate befalls us. In
the beginning we lack not life only, but form.
Not form only, but spirit. We are blent in the
one great featureless indistinguishable mass. Then
a time came when the mass evolved spirit, spirit
evolved form, form evolved life. And now life
in its turn has evolved death. For not nature
only but man's being has its seasons, its sequence
of spring and autumn, summer and winter. If
someone is tired and has gone to lie down, we
do not pursue him with shouting and bawling.
She whom I have lost has lain down to sleep for
a while in the Great Inner Room. To break in
upon her rest with the noise of lamentation would
but show that I knew nothing of nature's
Sovereign Law. That is why I ceased to mourn."
    Chuang Tzu and Hui Tzu were strolling one

----

[1] Both his attitude and his occupation were the reverse
of what the rites of mourning demand.

day on the bridge over the river Hao. Chuang
Tzu said, " Look how the minnows dart hither
and thither where they will. Such is the pleasure
that fish enjoy." Hui Tzu said, " You are not a
fish. How do you know what gives pleasure to
fish ? " Chuang Tzu said, " You are not I.
How do you know that I do not know what
gives pleasure to fish ? " Hui Tzu said, " If
because I am not you, I cannot know whether
you know, then equally because you are not a
fish, you cannot know what gives pleasure to
fish. My argument still holds." Chuang Tzu
said, " Let us go back to where we started. You
asked me how I knew what gives pleasure to
fish. But you already knew how I knew it when
you asked me. You knew that I knew it by
standing here on the bridge at Hao."

When Hui Tzu was minister in Liang, Chuang
Tzu decided to pay him a visit. Someone said
to Hui Tzu, " Chuang Tzu is coming and hopes
to be made minister in your place." This
alarmed Hui Tzu and he searched everywhere in
Liang for three days and three nights to discover
where Chuang Tzu was. Chuang Tzu, however,
arrived of his own accord and said, " In the
South there is a bird. It is called *yüan-ch'u*.[1]
Have you heard of it ? This *yüan-ch'u* starts from
the southern ocean and flies to the northern

---

[1] Identified nowadays with the Argus pheasant, but
used by Chuang Tzu in a mythological sense.

ocean. During its whole journey it perches on no tree save the sacred *wu-t'ung*,[1] eats no fruit save that of the *lien*,[2] drinks only at the Magic Well. It happened that an owl that had got hold of the rotting carcass of a rat, looked as this bird flew by, and terrified lest the *yüan-ch'u* should stop and snatch at the succulent morsel, it screamed, ' Shoo ! Shoo ! ' And now I am told that you are trying to ' Shoo ' me off from this precious ministry of yours."

Once when Chuang Tzu was walking in a funeral procession, he came upon Hui Tzu's tomb, and, turning to those who were with him, he said, " There was once a wall-plasterer who when any plaster fell upon his nose, even a speck no thicker than a fly's wing, used to get the mason who worked with him to slice it off. The mason brandished his adze with such force that there was a sound of rushing wind ; but he sliced the plaster clean off, leaving the plasterer's nose completely intact ; the plasterer, on his side, standing stock still, without the least change of expression.

Yüan, prince of Sung, heard of this and sent for the mason, saying to him, ' I should very much like to see you attempt this performance.' The mason said, ' It is true that I used to do it. But I need the right stuff to work upon, and the

[1] The kola-nut tree.
[2] Identified nowadays with the Persian Lilac.

partner who supplied such material died long ago.'

Since Hui Tzu died I, too, have had no proper stuff to work upon, have had no one with whom I can really talk."

THE END